IF MOUNTAINS DIE

Moon over Dixon, south of Taos

Text by JOHN NICHOLS

Photographs by WILLIAM DAVIS

IF MOUNTAINS DIE

A New Mexico Memoir

W. W. Norton & Company
New York • London

Grateful acknowledgment is made to Delacorte Press and Seymour
Lawrence for permission to reprint "I'm Explaining a Few Things"
excerpted from the book *Selected Poems* by Pablo Neruda, translated by
Alastair Reid, edited by Nathaniel Tarn. Copyright © 1970 by Anthony
Kerrigan, W.S. Merwin, Alastair Reid, and Nathaniel Tarn. Copyright
© 1972 by Dell Publishing Co., Inc. Reprinted by permission of
Delacorte Press / Seymour Lawrence.

Library of Congress Cataloging-in-Publication Data
Nichols, John Treadwell, 1940–
If mountains die : a New Mexico memoir/
text by John Nichols : photographs by William Davis.
Originally published : 1st ed. New York : Knopf, 1979
1. Taos Region (N.M.)—Description and travel.
2. Taos Region (N.M.)—Pictorial works.
3. Nichols, John Treadwell, 1940–
I. Davis, William, 1943–   II. Title.
F802.T2N5   1994
978.9′ 53—dc20   94-2243

ISBN 0-393-31159-7

Printed in Hong Kong

W.W. Norton & Company, Inc.
500 Fifth Avenue, New York, N.Y. 10110
W.W. Norton & Company Ltd.
10 Coptic Street, London WC1A 1PU

1 2 3 4 5 6 7 8 9 0

For the moon, the rocks, the land,
our hope — these, I feel, shall endure.
WILLIAM DAVIS

For Andrés Martínez,
Bernabé Chávez, Pacomio Mondragón, and Paul Valerio;
and for all the men and women like them
whose generous lives have long enriched this valley.
JOHN NICHOLS

Taos Mountain

As if by design, I arrived in Taos, New Mexico, almost the same day as John Nichols. That fall I would meet John briefly when I took a hitchhiker by his house to retrieve some belonging which had been left there. Then we would both spend the next several years involved in our separate personal ordeals, eventually refocusing on Taos and settling in here.

Taos has always impressed me with the beauty of its setting; a beauty I have come to think of as a result of a rare combination of mystical and human elements. The mountain is, of course, a major focal point and certainly enthralls one with its near-supernatural moods, as do the gorges and vistas to the west and south; but it is equally true that the impact of human habitation has played an essential role in shaping the valley itself.

Over the centuries first the Indian and then the Spanish peoples have created, with little more than earth, hands, and simple tools, a system of fields, orchards, and irrigation ditches and an indigenous architecture that must rank with those found anywhere. Depending on weather, season, and vantage point, one can seem to be in the Far East, rural England or Europe, the Mediterranean, the Near East, or even the southwestern United States.

This mixture, then, of the divine and the human in its landscape, the cultural diversity of peoples, and the burgeoning twentieth-century problems encroaching upon all make this area a crucible for life and thought, reducing this to a human dimension which can be dealt with more directly. With this in mind, John and I have undertaken to meld our individual responses to a place and time into as direct a statement as possible in the hope of awakening others to some of the responsibilities facing us all in the struggle toward new solutions to the human condition.

WILLIAM DAVIS
Taos, July 1977

If these mountains die,
where will our imaginations wander?
If the far mesas are leveled,
what will sustain us in our quest to be larger than life?
If the high valley is made mundane by self-seekers and
careless users, where will we find another landscape
so eager to nourish our love?
And if the long-time people of this wonderful country are
carelessly squandered by Progress, who will guide us
to a better world?

Sunrise from the lower Ranchos Valley rim

IF MOUNTAINS DIE

January sunrise, Taos Mountain

PRELIMINARY OBSERVATIONS

For the most part, my people come from towns, perched on the edges of two continents, overlooking the Atlantic Ocean. Having that vast seascape available within a stone's throw of their lives is important to their sense of time and place; it helps give them a strong cultural and historical identity. Most of my own life I never lived very far from the sea. Much of the rich tradition giving purpose to my blood is connected with sailing vessels and man-o'-war birds; with Breton fishermen and Salem sea captains; with the terns that wheel above sand dunes on Fire Island.

But for the last eight years I have lived in the shadow of northern New Mexico's high mountains, in a tough, semi-arid valley, surrounded by wide vistas of sagebrush mesa land and bordered on the west by a deep river gorge, a thousand miles from the sound of pounding breakers. I thought at first I would experience a discomfort from being trapped inland, so far from every reinforcement that mere access to beaches and water craft has meant to me. Yet, to my surprise, since I arrived in Taos in 1969 I have never had a longing for the Atlantic shore.

Whatever gifts of mood, space, and love the ocean once gave me, these southern Rockies have conjured up also. I can stand in my back field, gazing at the nearby peaks, feeling as centered as I ever felt on the threshold of an ocean. I can get my bearings against the silhouette of these Sangre de Cristos as easily as once I could reaffirm a cultural and physical balance against the sound of South Shore waves.

The bulk of these mountains is oceanic. In the place of whales, sharks, and porpoises they have mountain lions, elk, and bears. Their currents and reefs are beautiful meadows, talus slopes, thick forests, and streams full of trout. Their albatrosses and sea gulls are buzzards, ravens, and golden eagles.

Weather tumbles out of the mountains just as it rolls off the changing sea. Like the sea, these mountains can be dangerous, sudden, inexplicable — they can engulf and kill easily, then roll over and seem as gentle and as compassionate as a summer meadow: and you wonder how ever you could have feared them.

The mysteries and the myths involved with the Atlantic I have known are like the ballads and the superstitions raised by the Sangre de Cristos. And, as does the ocean, these mountains give the people who live in or near them an especially majestic perspective that helps to enlighten their daily struggles, and offers them the chance, if they will take it, to be larger than life.

So I have never felt at all trapped by this inland landscape. In fact, every day I feel the same way I have always felt when living on the brink of oceans.

Sometimes, however, I could throttle myself for being drawn to this strange patch of the Southwest I inhabit. Yesterday was April 20, 1977. As I wrote the preceding section, an early-spring blizzard howled. The dirt roof of my quaint adobe house leaked in a half dozen places. My neighbor's black Angus cattle thundered about the yard, trampling children's bicycles, smashing the dog pen, eating fragile rose bushes I have tended carefully for eight years. They also destroyed the only ungullied portion of my mud driveway that took ages to cultivate — a small section directly underneath the seven-foot-high basketball hoop. It used to be a ten-foot-high hoop, but last year the mayordomo of my front-field acequia backed into it after warning me I had better shoot all the muskrats honeycombing my ditch bank, causing water to illegally irrigate the half-acre front field.

The battle with my neighbor's obstreperous cows has been going on for three weeks now, ever since his dozen Angus commenced calving. Like rabbits, the calves squeeze through openings in the barbed-wire fence even a gopher would not essay. Immediately nervous, their enormous mothers then anxiously plow right through the wire to rejoin their insouciant offspring. At night sometimes I can hear the nervous bellowing of a cow trying to call back its calf from my side of the fence. Obliviously, the calves gambol around, eating my rich grass — why should they return to my neighbor's overgrazed plot? In fact, *everybody* over there is hungry. All day, every day, it seems, that black herd just stands in a row at the fence, gazing hungrily at my juicy green goodies. I feel like a rich kid with his pockets full of candy strutting through the ghetto. So at night the calves refuse to rejoin their mothers, and pretty soon the bellowing stops. Then I hear ancient cedar fence posts snapping — and rusty barbed-wire twangs — as eight hundred pounds of moronic bovinity enters my territory. By morning, the entire gang surrounds my little mud house in the beautiful seven-thousand-foot-high Taos Valley. They urinate on my VW bus (with its taped-over side window, spider-webbed front windshield, and 175,000-mile track record in life), chew on my Jockey underwear hanging on the line, and munch on the fragile branches of tiny greengage plum trees I've been nursing along for almost a decade.

Leaping out of bed, I hurl sticks and stones, I scream and shout, I spend an hour herding them all back home. Then I dig a new posthole, cram in a new post, repair broken barbed strands with baling wire, and even string up sections of old chicken wire where the calves are most obviously penetrating. Exhausted from the effort, I storm furiously through the sickening adobe glop that is northern New Mexico's answer to tar-pit ecology, and sit down at the typewriter, my sporadic clacking accompanied by raindrops plopping into various tin pots arranged about the dwelling. Ten minutes later the cows have created another break in the fence. Popping a digitoxin for my arrhythmic heart, I grab one of my kids' BB guns and plunge outdoors again, thanking God in some small rational part of my brain that the Daisy peashooter is not a .30-06 or, more to the point of how I'm feeling, an elephant gun or a bazooka! Fifteen minutes later, the cows are gone again, and I stumble breathlessly back inside, groping for an Aminodur Dura-Tab — that's what I take for asthma.

And I'm only thirty-six years old.

And I was perfectly healthy (if you discount being on the brink of a nervous breakdown) when I arrived in northern New Mexico in the summer of 1969.

Today, Thursday, April 21, 1977, the sun came out for a moment. I raced into Taos Hardware for roofing cement and saturated fiber to repair all the holes overhead before it rained, snowed, or hailed again. On the roof, I shuddered to observe what the ravages of winter had accomplished. Everywhere, the thin layer of goofily rippled tar paper covering eight inches of dirt riddled with a super strain of vertiginously breeding ants was cracked and bleeding water. A small rain lake covered the kitchen, where the roof was cleverly constructed years ago by a sadist who wanted a large water reserve overhead so that he could shower (while cooking his meals) for days after any cloudburst. Just to make sure water will collect on the roof and seep into every puncture in the rotting tar paper, the entire flat area is bordered by a foot-high, totally useless adobe firewall.

To make doubly sure all the indigenous flat-topped dirt roofs like mine will leak profusely, drainage is provided by only one or two tin canales protruding from the firewall. These are usually blocked by ice, or by leaves and twigs blown off the surrounding cottonwoods, hence their real historical function is to impede, rather than facilitate, drainage.

Today I gingerly climbed atop my anarchical dwelling and perched on a firewall for a moment, gazing into my neighbor's field at his hungry cattle. I thought how satisfying it might be to pull a Texas Tower massacre on that herd. Then I went to work patching the holes, the flashing, the firewalls, the canales. As I worked, a repugnant odor drifted up to me. At first I paid it no mind, assuming it was drainage from my kitchen and bathroom sinks and tubs fermenting in the front field. You see, a pipe exits from the house just under the kitchen sink, emerges into daylight fifteen feet away, crosses the Pacheco irrigation ditch, and dumps all the bath water into a healthy little clump of timothy and crabgrass. Only the toilet empties into a septic tank strategically located ten feet from the west wall of the house and ten feet from the east bank of the Pacheco ditch. The tank itself is lovingly cradled in the roots of two cannibalistic Chinese elm trees. And the water level in that area is about two feet below the surface. If you flush the toilet more than once a day, the septic tank overflows. If it rains, the septic tank overflows. If we have late-spring blizzards after an early-spring thaw, the septic tank overflows.

Which was the odor I smelled from my dirt roof today as I was patching the wounds of winter.

Given the situation, we have a high-class concrete outhouse that is always in tip-top working condition.

Still, these tribulations often get to me, and I wonder: Why here? Why Taos? Why northern New Mexico? I mean, every time I enter my criminally potholed driveway behind the wheel of my decrepit VW bus, the odds are seven to five I won't even make it as far as the corrugated culvert that channels the waters of the Pacheco ditch under my driveway and into Tom Trujillo's property. Every time a butane-gas truck lumbers up my driveway to fill an aluminum-colored submarine with liquid gold that often costs seventy-five dollars a winter month to use, the odds are seven to one that its enormous wheels are going to squash one end of my corrugated culvert, causing the waters of the Pacheco ditch to slosh over the bank, flooding my driveway and causing even deeper potholes. Then I must dig out the culvert with pickaxes and shovels and crowbars and spend an afternoon prying the mouth open with a scissors jack, so that Pacheco ditch waters can continue flowing uninterruptedly through my place to downstream users who would storm by toting cocked rifles if I allowed the culvert to stay squashed for any length of time.

Such hassles in this land of adobe nirvana often have me apoplectic. After all, this is the United States of North America, and I'm a middle-class citizen — a middle-class *white* citizen, no less — I got it all going for me. Just by snapping my fingers I should be able to wind up in an existence so genteel that when the revolution comes and they inspect my hands for calluses I'll go up against the wall so fast they won't even have time to ask me for my Social Security number.

Yet I have a quirk inside. I kind of like it when the natural world clobbers our technological universe. So what if hurricanes, earthquakes, mosquitoes, and idiot cattle make my life miserable? *Thank God nature can still kick me and all my gadgets in the teeth!*

Still, this has been a brutal winter. If I have loved the last six months, I have hated them also. I'm tired of being intimidated by the nasty grandeur of the thirteen-thousand-foot-high Sangre de Cristo Mountains. On the day before Easter three weeks ago, as I sat on my portal in seventy-degree sunshine begging the gracious weather to heal my winter blisters, I thought: I'll never do another winter in this godforsaken place. I'm too old. To hell with it. If Hemingway could write in Key West and Cuba, why not me? No more of this crap, I can't take it any more. I'll be dead by the age of forty if I continue to live in the North. It's costing me twelve grand a year to live at a poverty, subsistence level! It's been so cold my chickens haven't laid an egg for six months — I'm pouring grain into a bottomless pit. And I'm surrounded by packs of wild dogs and rabid skunks that will slaughter my entire flock in the wink of an eye some night when a gale-force April wind knocks over the hingeless chicken-pen door. It's too brutal, too cruel, I'm a fool, why fight it any longer?

Adiós, Nuevo Mejico: Hello, Dixie!

And yet where else in this country can a natural revenge so thoroughly take the measure of arrogant folks like me? There's real poetic justice in the job winter often does on the Taos Valley. In fact, when late-May frosts murder my apple blossoms for the fifth year in a row, I feel almost as euphoric as I felt in 1955 when the old Brooklyn Dodgers finally hammered the unbeatable Yankees. And when I sat on my firewall today almost in tears, I also had to chuckle.

Spring storm from Pilar Hill

Spring flood, Ranchos de Taos

And I love this wounded valley for precisely the same reasons that I often hate it: it is one of the few places I have ever been that I have truly taken personally.

So after I patched the roof and taped a note across the toilet — DON'T USE THIS HEAD, USE THE OUTHOUSE, PLEASE! — and hammered together the dog-pen door the cows had trampled yesterday, I went into the back field and performed a ritual that often calms me down. From the center of that small patch of brome, I stared at Taos Mountain. It always soothes me, that mountain. It is the most personal geological formation I have ever experienced. I feel closer to it than to any mountain I have ever climbed, from Monadnock in New Hampshire to Pyramid Peak in the high western sierras. I'm not even sure I know the real name for the mountain. Nor do I think I'll go out and ask somebody in order to have it down correctly in this book. The mountain overlooks Taos Pueblo, Taos proper, and all the surrounding villages: El Prado, Los Colonias, Upper and Lower Ranchitos, Cañon, Ranchos de Taos, Talpa, Llano Quemado, Los Córdovas, Cordillera. Behind it to the north rises bald, majestic Vallecitos. To the right, slightly northeast, stands New Mexico's highest mountain, Wheeler Peak. Though often I have hiked a trail passing several hundred feet below Wheeler's summit, never yet have I taken the brief detour that would have carried me to the top. I was always too intent on reaching Bear Lake, a profoundly turquoise, square-shaped lake centered in a magnificent alpine bowl whose southern slopes are bisected by the northern boundary of Taos Pueblo land. The ridges to the south of Bear Lake are darkened by Taos Mountain's evening shadows. The outlet stream from Bear Lake empties into the sacred Blue Lake stream that circles in front of the unique guardian mountain, and eventually travels between the two main Pueblo compounds. Five miles farther on, the Pueblo River runs by my house, only a few yards west of my front field.

Most of the land from which this special peak rises belongs to the Taos tribe, so I have never hiked that land. And in a way I hope I never will. Right now the unique mass of its powerful but friendly shape is perfect. If I ventured too close its overall beauty might melt into its own trees; its power, for me, might dissolve as it became less than the sum of all its parts. Accepting the mountain and its moods for a magician, I have no desire to learn how the tricks are performed. If an illusion of wholeness makes it special, then I will guard that illusion as one of the more precious gifts I have been granted. Distinctly privileged, I feel, living so near, yet forced to maintain a respectful distance.

Always over me or beside me, the mountain inhabits almost every landscape defining my days. If I visit friends at the Pueblo, it loses shape, growing top-heavy and elliptical — I am too close. Triangular ridges, outcroppings, and canyons traveling up its slopes admit too real dimensions. I feel more comfortable when I can drop back, allowing topography to dissolve into flatter planes, becoming part of a single impressive bulk, more of a symbol, I suppose, than a living thing.

Always, the mountain shapes any landscape I am in. Tiny or enormous, it claims the heart of every panorama here, always attracting the eye. From the town dump on the flat mesa land north of Taos, the mountain surges slowly out of a treeless mauve expanse like a powerful, benevolent creature rising from the sea. From my back field the mountain hovers protectively over the tiny Ranchitos community in which I live — a few mud houses, corrals and haystacks, some trailers, and a simple adobe church with a wooden bell tower. In town, robbed of a natural foreground, the mountain shrinks, inundated by motel, hotel, gas station, bank, and restaurant signs. Yet fifteen miles farther south, seen from the rim of the Rio Grande Gorge above a tiny village called Pilar, the mountain resides at the center of a stunning panorama. Taos evening lights twinkle insignificantly at the base of the wide peak like a thin line of phosphorus splashed at the foot of an enormous oceanic wave.

My eyes, and the eyes of all Taoseños, are forever attracted to the mountain. Nobody can travel the valley without centering off its bold presence. It is the central symbol in our lives to which the eye is always drawn. Some of us may take it for granted, yet in our subconscious it breathes heavily, an exclusively solid shape in the otherwise ever-changing, sometimes ugly, often beautiful, and too often unfortunate landscape through which we travel.

All weather entering or leaving the valley is defined by Taos Mountain. All calculations of weather seem to begin or to end around the mountain. On sunny spring days, warm enough to eliminate a piñon haze from town fires, breezy enough to prohibit smog from Albuquerque or from electric generating plants two hundred miles westward, the outline of the snow-powdered mountain is etched so sharply against the unreal acrylic blue sky that its lucidity can make you dizzy. When late-afternoon rusty sunlight settles against this most perfect of Sangre de Cristo hills, I feel the mountain is somehow submerged in stifling amber, calmly unable to breathe. Summer thunderheads crash ineffectually around the mountaintop like naughty kids buzzing a deaf, dumb, and blind child placidly smiling. And when fresh snow powders the valley and its surrounding forests, Taos Mountain shapes the white powder, as it shapes all weather, into a nearly perfect mood.

Occasionally, the clear winter light of fresh snow in this valley is so sharp it makes you cry out in pain. Or do I mean that you cry out from the lack of pain? Whatever the case, the real mood of our land and our natural phenomena is forever unerringly translated by Taos Mountain. For an area of such poverty and sorrow as is contained in the small villages of this high plain, the moods transcribed by Taos Mountain are surprisingly lucid, straightforward, hopeful. Nothing savage emanates from those cool slopes. Beige mists, dramatic crepuscular lights, thunderheads, and sheet lightning — all weather gains a hopeful perspective within the context of Taos Mountain. Its presence can only ameliorate the human condition.

As distinct, and as lovely, and as constant as Hokusai's Fuji, Taos Mountain is always a historical, emotional, visual starting point. If I feel sad, angry, euphoric, or insulted, the mountain always provides a relevant reference point, soothing, enhancing, or poignantly stabilizing my mood.

It holds together all the convoluted phenomena, patterns, and people of my home terrain.

Sometimes I feel that it directly keeps me from falling apart.

They say it draws back folks who have strayed.

They say it casts spells and prevents people from leaving.

Because of its significant shape, and because of its position in the valley, the mountain is the symbol for all that has ever happened or ever will happen here.

Its weight and shape always at least momentarily forge in me a calm heart.

Which is what can happen in my Taos back field when the roof leaks, and the septic tank overflows, and an April blizzard mugs my springtime with the crass brutality of a Mafia hit man.

November storm seen from Lower Ranchitos

Part **II**

ROOTS

A personal odyssey almost always begins long before that first step on the mythical journey of a thousand miles. Often roots that end up sluggishly searching for nourishment in desert soil began their growth more than two hundred years ago in a wet country by the side of an ocean. And the April nighttime cry of a Taos, New Mexico, killdeer in 1977 may have been heard first a hundred years ago by a great-grandfather on Long Island's southern shore, almost drowned by the Atlantic's roar.

"But how did you ever wind up in Taos?" people are constantly asking.

Jokingly, I usually begin my reply by saying, "Well, we wanted to get out of New York City, so we just threw a dart at a map of the United States, and here is where it landed."

Then I fumfer, toeing the earth, and dispense with a slew of sociological explanations that have some relevance to the case, but don't really tell the story.

There has got to be something else, going deeper, traveling farther back. When you wind up in a place that becomes a real home, you cannot simply attribute your arrival to casual accident, not in this nation of inveterate rovers. And when the place is so much of a home that almost immediately the land back East, where you did most of your growing up, looks like a foreign and cluttered planet covered with sickly green mold, you cannot cavalierly slough off this arid, wide-open territory as just another casual watering spot in the musical chairs of life.

One of the oldest and most important human drives is to locate, return to, stake claims upon the country of one's origins. These origins are physical, psychic, spiritual. Many of us forgot them generations ago —perhaps our forefathers, or our "melting pot" politicians, forgot our roots for us: and in a lifetime we never discover them again. Others among us are luckier: our people protected these sacred origins, sometimes by refusing to lose a native language or to sell an old house or a piece of land . . . sometimes by saving letters, diaries, old photographs . . . and sometimes by passing down, from one generation to the next, stories, history, and a special sensibility —approaching instinct– to land, politics, religion that becomes almost a genetic trait in the blood.

I set sail for this place, then, many generations ago.

And I cannot lose it now, for I have always had it. It is as strong in me as the stone that rolls from the top of the mountain to the bottom of the gorge. it is as swift in me as the *darting swallows: it is as inevitable as the snow falling past my window. Before I even knew the name of this place I could have proven to you that it had always existed in my heart, and in the hearts of my family that went before me. It is as immaterial in me as a dream, and as solid as sunshine and horses. That star, my star, has always been suspended exactly above this spot on earth: its shadow, the size and brightness of a dime, contains the mystery of my unique, and universal, heritage. I have known that crab apple tree outside my window all of my life, and all of my father's life, and all of his father's life before that. There is a continuity in the blood that transcends geography, language, skin color, time. In 1924, in Castle Hot Springs, Arizona, my maternal great-grandfather, writing in his native French, began a poem by saying: "Arizona skies, your splendor haunts me." So I embrace ravens, magpies, killdeer, my neighbors, their sheep, the mountains. My brothers speak many languages. In Taos I learn new superficial statistics that differentiate slightly the customs here from the customs over there, but deep down I have always understood the pattern of clouds over these tiny pastures. And I have played these same tunes before on my mother's guitar, on a great-grandfather's clarinet.*

When I got here, finally (when my body caught up to the rest of me), my life became a victory.

My mother's side of the family came from the northern coast of Brittany. My great-grandfather was a melancholy and beautiful writer called Anatole Le Braz. He wrote many stories and poems about the superstitious peasants and fishermen of that misty, bewitching territory. My father's side of the family hails from Salem, Massachusetts, and the South Shore of Long Island. There are whalers in the Salem crowd, merchant sea captains, also an ancestor who was executed as a witch. Down south on the Island, another direct ancestor was William Floyd. He lived in Mastic, centered almost exactly at that point where the eastern channel of Moriches Bay meets the western estuaries of the Great South Bay, and Fire Island is only a short canoe paddle awey. Among other things, William Floyd was a Revolutionary War general. And he signed the Declaration of Independence for New York.

I grew up spending my summers in the spare Puritan house that man's father built and roaming the six hundred acres of forest land, grain fields, and salt meadows my grandmother had clung to stubbornly despite efforts to tax the estate out of existence or condemn it for an atomic desalinization plant. In recent years, determined to keep the land intact, belligerent Floyds, Nicholses, Welds, and other assorted Puritan gangsters scrapped hard pulling the political strings necessary for donating the Mastic house and surrounding virgin territory to the federal government, provided it declare the old house a historic monument and maintain the surrounding land as a wildlife preserve and public park. It is hoped that the house and land will now be protected in perpetuity, a small bauble of green surrounded by superhighways, shopping centers, and tract houses.

The natural world has always been a magic territory for members of the Nichols, Floyd, Le Braz clans. The grandfather after whom I am named was a noted zoologist, biologist, ornithologist. Among other accomplishments, he founded *Copeia*, the journal of the American Ichthyologists and Herpetologists Society, and for many decades was Curator of Fishes at the American Museum of Natural History in New York City. Before reaching his twenties, he had already sailed in square-rigged ships around Cape Horn. In treacherous southern seas he caught flying fishes in a net, made numerous observations on Portuguese men-of-war, and studied albatrosses. Occasionally he captured these large birds by trailing a line baited with salt pork in the wake of his ship. The hook caught, but did not penetrate, a slight hollow in the upper mandible — it was necessary to keep the line taut while reeling the birds in. Occasionally they would take to the air when hooked, drifting like obstinate kites. And I've often pictured that tall, gaunt, pipe-smoking man, as I remember him from childhood days, dressed in a crumpled fedora and wrinkled old suit, standing on the aft deck of a full-masted sailing vessel, reeling in those enormous birds from out of the iceberg-green air.

My own father followed in his old man's footsteps. He grew up curiously inspecting every inch of the Mastic land, getting to know all the trees, birds, flowers, foxes, and sandpipers on the place. Most of his time was spent outdoors, tramping on land and along beaches, clinically and joyously acquainting himself with nature. The rest of his hours were spent in various aquatic vehicles, getting to know by heart the waters of Moriches Bay.

Like everyone else in the family, my dad had plenty of rabbit in his blood at an early age. And by his late teens, having followed the kind of impulse that would later launch me in the same direction, my old man found himself "out West." Traveling alone on horseback, he ran traplines in Nevada, building up a small-mammal collection for the American Museum of Natural History in New York. And I grew up listening to his legends from that time. In Reno, Nevada, my dad once sat down to cards with Pretty Boy Floyd . . . or so he claims. Dismounting from a horse on another occasion, he was bit on the knee by a rattlesnake. Pop slashed open the knee with a hunting knife, sucked out the poison, and saved his life . . . or so he says, with a Wry Chuckle.

But hasn't he got the scar to prove it?

Around the same time my father was playing five-card stud with famous American gangsters and learning "Little Joe the Wrangler" on his guitar, my mother, Monique Robert Le Braz, was heading for the U.S.A., a southwestern destination in her travel plans. She arrived in New York accompanied by her step-grandmother, an American woman who was the sister of the late robber baron Henry P. Davison, a partner of J. P. Morgan and former American envoy to Poland. They arrived in this country about the same time that my great-grandmother's nephew, F. Trubee Davison, Hoover's Assistant Secretary of War, was succeeding Henry Fairfield Osborn as president of the American Museum of Natural History, where my father's father inhabited a wonderfully unkempt cubicle jammed full of ichthyological papers and dozens of urine-brown bottles containing pickled fishes.

Through such convoluted connections were the son of New England Puritans and the granddaughter of "the Bard of Brittany" destined to meet and create an offspring who would one day wind up in northern New Mexico as the semi-Marxist-Leninist propaganda arm for a group of quixotic Spanish-speaking septuagenarians locked in mortal combat with the United States government over the preservation of their water rights, their land, their culture, their very historical roots.

My mother's last few months before her departure for Santa Fe were far different from the emotional turmoil that occupied my own life prior to ditching Manhattan thirty-seven years later. In December of 1932 she attended a dinner and dance at the Ritz-Carlton for debutante Dorcas Oakly Ferris. A week later, at another dinner dance, for Mrs. Dwight Whitney Morrow's daughter Constance, she met Anne Morrow Lindbergh. My mother bought evening dresses at Saks, and had her hair cut there also. Her Aunt Kate (Mrs. Henry P. Davison) threw a house party in her honor at the North Shore estate — my mother's American home — called Peacock Point. Newspaper cameramen publicized the occasion by photographing Monique in her white velvet dress. She bounced through all this social folderol like a good-humored lamb: her diary is full of laughter, enthusiasm, a complete sweetness and innocence that belie the Depression around her. In fact, her good-natured naïveté and acceptance of wealth occasionally seem almost criminal to me these many years later. Yet her passion was ultimately winning. And one night in the Peacock Point mansion she wrote: "Santa Fe, the Grand Canyon, Death Valley, and Los Angeles — how wonderful all those words sound. They are like the promised land to me!"

On January 1, 1933, my mother boarded the Twentieth Century Chief for Santa Fe. Three days later she had a room at the Santa Fe La Fonda Hotel, out West at last. Writing in her diary just before going to sleep on January 4, Monique said: "From my bed I can see, through the open window, all the stars in heaven. Oh I am happy, happy, happy!"

Two days after that, my mother had a truly powerful experience. When I read it for the first time in her diary, I was startled, because nothing she had ever revealed to me in her writings up to that point had posited her as much more than a kind of goody two-shoes, a totally sweet and always smiling woman. The experience, as she recounted it, involved a Pueblo Indian family whom she had apparently met a year earlier during some cultural ceremonies in New York.

From her diary:

This day has been an unforgettable one for me. I have had an experience that is and will always be one of the outstanding ones of my life.

We started yesterday morning in a Harvey car with a very nice courrier and an even nicer cowboy driver, Russell. I sat by him and we left for San Ildefonso. The day was very cold, clear and sunny, the country we went through very beautiful. We saw the Black Mesa from a distance, then arrived in San Ildefonso. It looked absolutely deserted. I don't think we will see another Pueblo as lovely as this one. There are two plazas, the old and the new. The old one has a big cottonwood tree in the middle and little low houses around at the edges. It is really a big, big plaza and the houses are so far from the center and so quiet that it looks more like an open field than a plaza. We went to Maria and Julian's house and there inquired about Ogwa Pi's house. They told us it was on the plaza, so we went back and found it. As I was getting down from the car, across the plaza from somewhere came Ogwa Pi. He has not changed, only today he was at home, in his Pueblo, with his people. He is the most dignified person I have ever seen. And the way he talks is as dignified as the way he stands and walks. He shook hands with me and accepted one of the shells I had brought, then he turned to the house and said: "Entre." I went in alone with him, and found myself in a very neat, tidy, nice-looking room. By the fireplace stood a woman. She was not handsome and looked older than he, but she had the loveliest expression and smile, as Ogwa Pi said: "Mi mujer." She shook hands with me, and if ever anybody introduced his wife with as much pride and love, that was Ogwa Pi. He said he had to go to get ready for the dances but that I could stay here to wait and also the people who were with me if they wanted to. I asked him if he had received letters which I wrote him from France and, for an answer, his face twitched in something like a smile (though his wonderful eyes always stay the same, piercing you to the very bottom) and he said: "I wrote you once, too; the letter is in here" (pointing to a drawer); "it came back to me." Then he went and the rest came in. His little girl was there, too, and the oldest boy was playing outside. I gave his wife all the other things I had brought and she took them just as simply. Neither of them said anything or showed by their expression whether they were pleased or not and Tante Kate asked me if I didn't find them very unresponsive. Unresponsive! My goodness! If anybody ever was responsive it was those two, in their own manner. Why do you want thanks from people like that? It is all underneath. I understood and they understood and we knew what each other wanted to do, so what need to talk of it?

Finally we went out and, soon after, the first group of dancers came out to do the Eagle Dance. It was the same which I had seen in New York, but oh, what a difference. The beauty of this was overpowering, and when the courier came to me and said "Isn't it beautiful," I felt like shouting "Shut up," but instead ran away from her. No words can add to that beauty. Better look and stay quiet. The drumming and singing that accompanied the dancing was just right. We were the only strangers there, with a few other Indians watching and children playing marbles. That was all, and you felt so deeply that they were not doing that for anybody but their gods and themselves. That group finished and the other one came out for a Kiowa dance. Ogwa Pi danced in this one. On their backs they wore shields made of feathers and Ogwa Pi's was mostly made of the peacock feathers I sent him last year. When they had finished, the other ones came out again and so on, but we had to go for lunch. I went into the house to tell Ogwa Pi's wife that we were leaving but would be back after lunch. But before going I bought a painting of Ogwa Pi's from her and she gave me a photograph of that room with the family. She also showed me the dress she wears in dances with my ribbons sewed on. Then, as I was going, she put something in my hand and said, "Take this anillo." The anillo was a big beautiful ring of silver with a gorgeous turquoise. Being with them, I felt like them, and though I was overpowered I barely said thank you. We went for lunch at a little tea-place at the station at Otowi, near there, with a Miss Warner. The place belongs to Maria and Julian. We had a delicious lunch and went back to San Ildefonso right after it. I alone got down and went in. Ogwa Pi was not there but his wife said he had told her to send for him when I came, so she sent the boy. I could hear his bells and rattles as he drew near and then he came in the door in his full dance costume. He came over to the fireplace where I was and asked me how I liked the dances. It is a wonderful thing about them how anxious they are that I should be pleased and like their things. Then with his wife, he went over to a big chest,

Fall snowstorm above Arroyo Seco

opened it and took out a beautiful, long string of turquoise wampum. He turned and came straight to me, looking me in the eyes all the time, and he put it over my head and on my neck. My heart beat terrifically and I felt and knew he had just done something very grave and important. It was going through the deepest ceremony. It certainly was the most impressive one I have ever been through. He asked me when they would see me again and I said perhaps soon, perhaps not in a long, long time. He said, "We won't forget," and "Write us." And then, as I was turning the doorknob to go out, he asked me: "Do you like us?" I answered: "Very much," and his last words were "We like you." Never has anybody given me such a sense of a wonderful honor being put upon me as those three words were said. I went out and across to the car without breathing almost. It was all so sacred—

I like to pretend that perhaps at that same moment, six hundred miles away, a gangly and solitary teen-age boy — who would one day become my father — rounded a mesquite bush on horseback, or rode his mount loosely out of an arroyo, and reined in, gazing down upon perhaps one of the most magnificent sights he had ever seen. A wide desert rain lake, only inches deep but stretching for miles, and pockmarked with a thousand ducks, or maybe a flock of long-legged avocets. A visual experience so breathtaking that he may have gulped in air, unable to catch his breath for a moment, imprinting on my future consciousness (just as my mother was recording that precious moment at San Ildefonso) whatever mysterious code it is that guides us all, inevitably, into our original and unforeseeable destinies.

We moved often during my childhood, touching down in eight states and twice that many towns. I went through nearly a dozen schools — to quote one of the old man's favorite expressions — "like green corn through a cow." But a constant thread wherever we went, no matter how confused the family situation might be, was the visits to my grandmother's summer residence, William Floyd's paean to Puritan conservatism, the old white house in Mastic.

That house was the center of my history and my cultural roots for most of my early life. Every year of my childhood I eagerly awaited the moment when I could return there again: if only for a week, or for a month, an entire summer. The history of our family was contained there: in two-hundred-year-old portraits on the spare walls; in diaries of my aunts, and great-uncles, and other distinguished or totally bonkers relatives dating back to Revolutionary War times; in the attic Civil War uniforms relatives had worn; in the old trunks up there, one of which contained hundreds of *Harper's Weekly*'s from a century ago; in the gun room's useless flintlocks and other assorted weaponry with which we kids played cops and robbers.

In my early childhood a telephone never rang in that house. For light, we had kerosene lamps. I used mayonnaise jars for catching little brown bats that slept during the day behind the green shutters. I captured fireflies on a front lawn as big as a football field where rabbits grazed, oblivious to my shenanigans. Later, we collected some of those same rabbits from the lethal dungeon of the old icehouse floor where they had fallen, breaking their necks. Sometimes we children tugged saddles onto the peak of the icehouse roof and galloped two thousand miles . . . to Santa Fe, the Grand Canyon, Death Valley. Later, with my cousins, I learned to hunt at Mastic. We hid in tall *Fragmites* weeds bordering shallow ponds, and shot black ducks and mallards, widgeon, and teal that came into range. On icy December pre-dawns we loaded burlap sacks full of old wooden scaup decoys onto duckboats, and towed the narrow, camouflaged boats along thinly iced canals to the choppy, slate-gray waters of Moriches Bay. Upland shooting took place in fields of rye and barley cultivated by my uncle David Weld. And if the local foxes were off their feed, we had quail and pheasant galore.

At least once every summer, I traipsed through the woods to our family graveyard, where my mother, who died when I was two, is buried only a few feet away from the memorial tomb of William Floyd. On other century-old headstones, winged skulls grinned at me fiendishly. South of the cemetery fence, nearly lost among tangles of underbrush and honeysuckle, stood a half dozen carefully painted white wooden crosses carrying the first names of slaves who had died on the estate.

As a small kid at the Mastic house, I remember being awakened early by my old man. Heading out to check his traps, he invited me along. He was amassing a small-mammal collection for the Museum of Natural History. Thin, tall sticks sporting white rag pennants marked the location of each mousetrap in the wild field beyond the manicured lawn. Proudly, I toted his collecting pouch. Breathlessly, I anticipated our haul. Mist brooded heavily on the front lawn as if some Hollywood fog machine hidden behind the enormous linden, towering over the southwest corner of the house, had laid down an artificial mood so that I would remember the morning for all time. A stately ring-necked pheasant that had been quartering the lawn for tidbits melted away through the vapor. Crows were gathering silently over the distant tree line where forest began.

Entering the field, we approached the first trap. Squatting, my father carefully removed a plump, short-tailed, velvet-gray body and handed it over, informing me that it was a field mouse, *Microtus pennsylvanicus*. I thumbed it softly, then slipped it into the pouch. After that, for an hour we wandered through delicate lespedeza, inspecting the traps, occasionally removing a tiny victim. To see animals that close, to touch them, gave me an enormous thrill.

The mist lifted, a sea gull floated by overhead, Dad took my hand. I could have dissolved from the happy curiosity that threatened to burst my veins. We were by the edge of the woods, gazing at the old house floating in the quietly dissolving morning mood. A little farther along, spotting a box turtle, I gave a triumphant shout. From 1915 until his death, my grandfather marked the turtles found on the Mastic land. He kept records of every tortoise brought to him by family, friends, children. The one I located in 1945 had been found by my father in 1921, when he was five years old, and marked and registered accordingly. Twenty-three years later, when he was four years old, my son Luke spotted a box turtle beside the road near Mastic. Pulling over, we inspected the turtle: it had last been marked by my own father in 1932!

In the kitchen, after running the front-field traplines, we spread the day's take of field mice and house mice, moles and tiny shrews, onto the oilcloth-covered table. Dad taught me how to skin the mice, curing the pelts in fine cornmeal, stuffing the little creatures, and pinning them out as museum specimens on mounting boards. And the way I leaned over the old man back then, absorbed in his quiet, often wisecracking and humorous work, must have been much the same way my own children gathered around me decades later, watching as I laboriously skinned and stuffed birds that we had picked up from highway shoulders on our travels around New Mexico.

As I grew older, always moving around a lot, the William Floyd house at Mastic helped to keep me steady, even as the image of Taos Mountain helps to keep me balanced when I am on the road today. For that estate was the most precious and most dominating connection with nature I ever had. It also represented a continuity of generations — my real and tangible roots. I carried the sensation of belonging to a family, a race, and to history that it gave me wherever I went while growing up. Granted, I also have strong, less conscious identities with the somber seaside culture of Brittany and with a dozen seafaring generations out of Salem. But Mastic, as the most known quantity inherent in my roots, has given me the most palpable identity.

Two years ago, while fishing the Little Rio Grande about a half hour from my front door, a friend and I treed a bear cub. Never before had I seen such an animal in the wilderness. And as I stood in the gathering darkness at the foot of that pine peering up into its thick branches, I was moved by a curiously touching excitement. My imagination had received a special boost: all existence was suddenly worthwhile. Since then, I have seen no other bears along the streams I love to fish. But I never know. The possibility is always there, for I have seen the evidence that bears are around. I go through life holding the anticipation of seeing another bear close to my own essence: it is like the possibility of seeing a whale in the ocean. And that possibility makes beautiful the background of my everyday existence, it enhances and colors my dreams.

Mastic had possibilities like that.

January morning

Part III

THE ROAD TO TAOS

This is her land, her town, but she has never really lived here. Her parents were brought up here, and then they moved away from the northern mountains to California, leaving behind a tiny adobe near the river and the cottonwood grove. She was brought up in Califas, in places like Oakland's Jingletown. It was not an easy life: she had to deal with racism every step of the way. But she made it through college and became a teacher, and also a singer and composer of songs. Growing up, she heard stories of her father's birthplace in the small, impoverished northern New Mexico town. Finally, almost an adult, she made a pilgrimage to the North, and, once having seen it, swore to return. I am reminded of how, at the age of twenty-two, I finally arrived at my own French ancestral home town, a tiny fishing village called Port Blanc, in Brittany, on the northern coast of France. The tide dropped twenty, thirty feet every day, exposing seaweed and enormous boulders. The people were stern, superstitious, they drank a lot. Their houses were made of brick, spare and puritan: you took off your shoes at the door and put on slippers. They had their own language: they were very poor. Culturally, they were strong. Life revolved around the tiny port, the picturesque village, the shrouded sea.

My friend understands —but does not speak —Spanish, her native tongue. She can sing as beautifully as anyone I have ever heard. Her own songs are sometimes angry, sometimes lyrical, and bittersweet. They speak of her life, her family, racial conflict, her yearning for roots. In California she has done many benefits for the farm workers, César Chávez, AIM. Here, her contract at a local nightclub prohibits her from doing radical songs: nevertheless, in Spanish, she sings about Manifest Destiny, genocide, revolution.

There is so much life, so much laughter and vitality, so much confusion and tragedy in her blood.

For this moment there is a solid, sunshine-filled peace here on the hillside, among the juniper and piñon trees, overlooking her town, the valley where her ancestors farmed, intermarried, created legends, died. Smoke trickles from a chimney: somebody is irrigating. So-and-so's trailer burned up yesterday; the magpies are noisy. We can see her little house, the bright sun-symbol on the front façade. Her father is in the attic, insulating, making more rooms for the family. Her brother and his wife and two children have begun returning from California during the summer: they too would like to leave that promised land for good, and set up shop in their real home country.

"This is where I belong," she says. "This is where I am going to live. There's no place else for me to run to."

We sit on the hillside, singing funny songs to each other, hers from "Sesame Street," mine from Tammy Wynette. Then we are quiet, overlooking the calm valley.

"This is also the most beautiful place on earth," she says.

I have heard that from teen-agers here: and I have heard it from octogenarians who spent three quarters of their lives abroad, searching for something they never found, until, at last, they came back home.

I came out here for the first time at the age of sixteen to discover a territory destined to become my future home. That was twenty years ago, and I was about the same age my parents had been when each of them first set foot upon the inland territory of deserts, canyons, and rugged mountains that comprise the American West.

I had won a trip to a national student council conference in Roswell, New Mexico, by writing an essay on "What Democracy Means to Me." I did not triumph in a rousing competition among my fellow prep school essayists: quite the contrary. I think I was the only contestant who submitted an essay! No matter — any old ticket in a storm. Unfortunately, a few days before my scheduled departure, I received a collect telegram from the conference committee stating they hadn't received my school's registration fee for membership in the National Association of Student Councils, and therefore I couldn't attend the conference.

Talk about brokenhearted!

My father and I were living in a small Washington, D.C., apartment at the time: he was briefly in between marriages. We huddled together after that tragic telegram, me with bitter tears in my eyes. Pop said he had an extra hundred bucks he could front me if I still wanted to head out West and look around. I accepted his generosity. Three days later, carrying a letter of introduction to the director of the American Museum of Natural History's Southwest Research Station in Portal, Arizona, I took off.

That summer, as Richard Starkey might say, has loomed forever large in my legend. What happened out there changed my life. I left Washington, D.C., as a sixteen-year-old crewcut, white-bucks-wearing, all-American boy; I returned two months later sporting long hair swept back into a DA, a dusty old Levi's jacket, scuffed fruit boots, and a Spanish accent.

When I departed our nation's capital I carried forty dollars in cash, a picture of my prep school girl friend, and a lucky rabbit's foot in my pockets: I returned toting two hundred and fifty bucks earned as a volunteer smoke chaser in the Chiricahua Mountains, and a number of switchblade knives purchased in Agua Prieta, Old Mexico. Naturally, I had taken up smoking Camel cigarettes: in those days before Marlboro Country, what other brand was there? At the start of the summer, about the only sentence I could speak in Spanish was one taught to me by my old man when I was eleven: "Es necesario trabajar mucho para aprender el español." By summer's end, this vocabulary had been expanded a hundredfold, all of it funky and unprintable. Even now I can vividly remember a simple incident that occurred in Amarillo during a rest stop. Crossing the street, I halted abruptly to let pass an old Ford convertible crammed with local kids, one of whom flipped me a finger, shouting "Tomalo, puto!" as they careened by. For at least a decade thereafter, anytime I really wanted to invectimize anybody getting on my case, I just cranked up the old bird and sneered, "Tomalo, puto!" And, man, they *understood!*

Talk about mileage from those two months. In my own heart, in my imagination, in all the bullshit I slung to eager listeners over the following decades, I played it up more than any other experience that had occurred previously, or that has taken place since. For going out West that first time was the kind of adventure in which nothing could go wrong, and the gods were willing to grant me a gift that would shape my future, forging longings I could never suppress.

As soon as my bus pulled into Albuquerque, I bought a four-dollar cowboy hat and an eight-dollar switchblade. Then, according to my diary of that time, I helped an Indian kid lug around newspapers he was selling, saw ". . . *The Wayward Bus* with Jayne (spelled S-E-X) Mansfield in it," and after that purchased a book on how to speak Spanish. In Santa Fe, I had an enormous steak, French fries, and salad for eighty-seven cents. With a letter of introduction to the brother of a gentleman farmer I had worked for in Virginia, I hit Taos at 10:30 p.m., checked into the La Fonda Hotel on the Plaza, and lay on my bed with the door open, listening to a ragtime piano player banging away downstairs.

For a week I stayed in Taos, living with a hyperactive,

ebullient child-man named Justin Locke, who worked my ass off in exchange for room and board. And he showed me some Taos sights to boot.

Nowhere does my Runyonesque diary mention the Taos Mountain. But it does recall jackrabbits and the famous Ranchos de Taos church being mud-plastered by dozens of mysterious women. On the mesa behind Justin's house, tiptoeing gingerly because I expected a rattlesnake behind every tuft of sage, I collected ancient Indian pottery shards, photographed my first cactus — a tiny prickly pear — and, in the heart of the desert high country where less than twelve inches of rain falls annually, I heartily cursed the mosquitoes.

Even today an occasional case of equine encephalitis scares people half to death. In the thirties, every small community in northern New Mexico had problems with malaria. And thanks to prairie dogs, to poverty, and also, no doubt, to lousy drainage of what little damp area there is, we New Mexicans top the U. S. A.'s plague statistics every year!

Back in 1957, at Justin Locke's house, I also chopped alfalfa, hauled rocks for a flagstone floor, sanded and sealed the cracks in a homemade swimming pool, killed weeds and helped irrigate, transplanted trees, hammered out the mud of a garden wall to make an archway, fixed cracks in the pump house, painted a wall, tarred the roof, helped install some electric wiring, and cut the lawn.

Time permitting, I also visited the Pueblo and the famous mysterious painting in the Ranchos church called "The Shadow of the Cross." One night, in a house down the hill, an old man named Romero resined up his bow and played the fiddle for us. At a town gallery I saw an exhibit of Dorothy Brett paintings. But the best time I had during my first and only week in Taos that summer was just lying around the house and its environs during the siesta hour, quietly playing the guitar while I gazed out over the Ranchos-Talpa Valley from my vantage point on the Llano Quemado ridge. Sometimes I lay in a hammock strung on the front portal and lazily watched the valley, or charted the moods of weather occurring around the mountains and the sagebrush plain to their west.

I still believe that house and its view to be among the most beautiful I have ever known. And when Justin sold it a few years ago, after toiling for almost twenty-five years in that Gar-den of Eden suspended in space, it felt to me as if he were selling an important part of me too.

Over the years Justin had carefully renovated the old adobe. It was cool and dark inside, with fireplaces, and narrow arched doorways that made you duck passing through. Big cottonwoods and aspen trees lined the back irrigation ditch. A few small, rich lawns surrounded the house, their lush greenery shadowed by apple, plum, and apricot trees. Despite Justin's asthma, a terraced hillside dropping sharply into the valley from just beyond the front portal was planted with timothy, brome, and other grasses that rippled in the breezes. And from that portal nothing blocked the view. You could see the Sangre de Cristo Mountains from Llano Quemado damn near up to Blanca Mountain behind Fort Garland, Colorado. Westward, across the Rio Grande Gorge, lay San Antonio Mountain on the road to Alamosa, Colorado. Even farther west stretched the hills by Tierra Amarilla, where one day Reies Tijerina would come to fame with his land-grant movement, in neighboring Rio Arriba County. Closer to home was the entire Ranchos-Talpa Valley, bisected by the Little Rio Grande. Uninterruptedly, the eye could sweep from the mouth of the eastern canyon through the communities of Llano, Talpa, and Ranchos, across the highway and west through Cordillera, Lower Ranchitos, and Los Córdovas, and then across the sagebrush mesa and the narrow gash of the Rio Grande Gorge, and far, far beyond, to Jicarilla Apache country, and maybe even to Arizona and Navajo land.

Twenty years later, the contained world below Justin's house is still fairly undeveloped. The valley is not deep enough to prohibit early-morning or late-afternoon sunshine, but you can still look down onto the backs of iridescent black-and-white magpies drifting over freshly cut fields and feel godlike. It's a clean valley; the patterns of tiny pastures, orchards, and willow groves, barbed-wire fence lines and dirt roads, are organic and comforting. Natural shapes and bisecting lines are complementary: all activity down there is generic, peaceful, reassuring. And if you lift your eyes only an inch, as I did long ago during the magic siesta hours, the entire Sangre de Cristo range travels north, snow-whitened even on a June day.

I felt I could jump off the ridge at that spot where Justin Locke had created his Eden and almost fly, sustained in a lavish buoyancy simply by the view.

Lower Valdez Valley

Tumbleweed in salt cedars

Instead, I reboarded a bus and headed south. During another layover in Albuquerque, I purchased a pair of twenty-dollar, white-toed, purple, gaudily tooled, knee-high, mule-ear boots, and bought a ticket for Rodeo, New Mexico.

"Rodeo, New Mexico — ?" The bus driver had never heard of it. For the record, I showed him a map, locating the town halfway between Lordsburg, New Mexico, and Douglas, Arizona. At 6 a.m. next morning a shuttle bus dropped me off smack dab in the middle of nowhere, in the heart of a heartless little desert.

Rodeo was — still is, for that matter — an old railroad trestle that carries no tracks, a few fading yellow caved-in railroad buildings, a couple of useless stock pens, a scattering of windmills. A few dozen enormous dead cottonwood trees lie around like fallen Goliaths. A bar, a general store, a few seedy houses complete the picture. Animas Mountains to the east; craggy cones of the Chiricahuas about ten miles immediately west. Portal, Arizona, which houses the American Museum of Natural History's Southwest Research Station, was in the Chiricahuas, so I hefted my heavy suitcase and started walking. Six miles later, in the hundred-degree heat, my tongue began swelling in my mouth. Had I been brave enough to glance skyward, I'm sure I would have seen buzzards circling. The first vehicle to come along — an ancient pickup driven by an old Spanish-speaking galoot — gave me a lift into the metropolis of Portal: one general store, a ranger station, a post office. I drank three Cokes, a quart of milk, and vomited for ten minutes. Then another Good Samaritan drove me to the Research Station, about four miles up the canyon in a picturesque little valley some twenty degrees cooler than the flatlands.

Gorged with orchards, meadowland flowers, and big old cottonwoods, scrub pine, and ponderosa, the valley had more flying, walking, crawling, fluttering, singing wildlife than I have ever seen concentrated in a single place since. Back East, a couple of ruby-throated hummingbirds at our flowers gave an enormous thrill. In this place, flocks of hummingbirds, some nearly as big as finches, crowded the open area between compounds. They were lined up on elm and cottonwood branches like New York City subway-token buyers, waiting to get a shot at the multiple feeders. Nearby, a large lizard colony occupied the center of the plaza. Behind the main house and dining room a swimming pool was surrounded by rich grasses. A dry creek bed close to the dining hall had a small flash flood every afternoon following cloudbursts higher in the mountains. And a lab right out of John Steinbeck's *Sweet Thursday* was so full of dusty menacing rattlesnakes in glass cages it squirmed.

As a favor to my father and grandfather, no doubt, the foreman assigned me a bed in the bunkhouse for hired hands: I could stick around awhile, working for room and board. I had just collapsed onto my bed without bothering to shuck my iridescent mule-ear boots when the head forest ranger came by, looking for a man to hike into the hills and locate a smoking tree and cut it down before the fire crowned out, costing the U.S. government ten million dollars in kickbacks from timber sales. The foreman sent him to me. "How old are you, son?" the ranger asked.

I told him: "Sixteen."

"Well, you got to be eighteen to earn a buck fifty around the clock as a Volunteer Smoke Chaser for the U.S. government," he said. "So I'm gonna ask you that question again. How old are you, son?"

"Eighteen, sir."

"Sign on the dotted line, Mr. Nichols."

Two hours after I had arrived at the Research Station, I found myself stumbling around the high country with a man whom I'll call Melvin Marcy, a big-bellied, balding fellow who used to be a "rassler" in traveling carnivals, and currently had aspirations to wind up "skinnin' the cat" on construction jobs over in Phoenix or Tucson. Two big axes over our shoulders, we were searching for a burning snag the lookout had spotted "right beside a major trail."

We found it all right, two hours later and about three miles off the trail in some of the roughest country going. But the tree was enormous. Even if we could have chopped it down, there would have been no way to keep the fire from spreading through the abundant brush. Reluctantly, we walked out to the Rustler's Park ranger station and picked up a Swedish bucksaw, a shovel, a pair of fire-fighting hoe-rakes called korticks, and some government issue C rations. Under a full moon at 10 p.m., we started back for the burning tree. The stars were so bright they seemed like fireflies dangling on threads inches above our heads.

At the start we could see a tiny flame miles away, halfway up a steep ridge at the top of a long shale slide. To get there necessitated dropping into canyons and climbing cliffs, hence we lost sight of the fire immediately. And then, despite that neon moon and the fluorescent stars, we lost track of the tree, and really began to flounder, backtracking, uselessly clawing up through brush to a hundred different knolls, trying to get our bearings again. In short order, we panicked. What if the tree crowned out and started a rampaging forest fire? Or suppose one of us suffered a rattlesnake bite? "This fuckin' country is so full of rattlesnakes it ain't even *funny!*" my partner groaned.

Then his heart attacks commenced. Mel toppled over gasping, drenched in sweat. His eyes bulged; his chubby lips were lead-colored. "My heart stopped!" he croaked. "I got a weak heart. Oh Lord, I'm gonna die! There ain't enough oxygen up here! I don't wanna die up here, oh Jesus Christ Almighty! *I don't wanna die!*"

"Get up," I whispered hoarsely. "You can make it. We're almost there. It's right over the next ridge. Don't die on me, please —"

"I can't carry all this equipment, John. Oh goddammit all to hell, I fear I'm a goner!"

"I'll carry your stuff, I don't mind!" I wailed. "Just please don't die on me, Mr. Marcy! We're almost there. Honest. I promise. It's right over the next hill —"

But it wasn't. We climbed, descended, doubled around, backtracked, gasped, gurgled, floundered. I was lugging two korticks, a shovel, two canteens, a Swedish bucksaw, and the C rations. Knuckles on both my hands were chopped raw on the sawteeth. Every time I cried ouch or seemed about to complain about hauling all that equipment, Mel crumpled into another thicket, apoplectic, lobster-faced, erupting. I kept begging him, "Please don't die!" because I couldn't cut down that tree alone and I didn't want to be blamed for a ten-million-dollar fire. I had only just arrived out West, for God's sake! And my twenty-dollar super-special genuine Rodeo Cowboyman's Association mauve-and-gold mule-ear footwear started falling apart as if it were made of cardboard instead of genuine all-American New Mexico cowhide!

Around 2 a.m., a virtual hardware store in one arm, practically dragging my fellow fire fighter with my other hand, I lucked into the bottom of the shale slide a hundred yards below the fiery pine. Mel gave a shout — "Hallelujah!" — and scrambled up the slide on all fours in two seconds flat. He collapsed at the base of the tree, instantly asleep. Hampered by all the utensils cluttering my arms, I could not make it up that final slope. For every frantic step forward, I slid two backward. In five minutes I had progressed twenty yards. I kept dropping a kortick, losing the shovel when I reached for the kortick: the sawteeth continued ripping my fingers; a handle stabbed me in the groin; my mule-ear boots filled up with pebbles. Any second now, going for a handhold, I'd grab a rock rattler instead of a stone, and that would be it — Eternity Junction! I cursed Melvin Marcy, I screamed at the burning tree overhead, I sobbed and blew my cool and bellowed for all the Chiricahuas to hear: *"I can't do it! Somebody help me!* HELP ME, GODDAMMIT ALL TO HELL ANYWAY!"

Eventually, I made it up the slide, and commenced pounding on Mel's chest. One eye opened: he stared at the teen-age madman hovering like the Angel of Death over his palsied, totally drained features. "We got to cut down the son of a bitch before it crowns out!" I sobbed.

"Go away, John. Go fuck a lame coyote."

Yanking Mel onto his feet, I shoved the saw handle into his hand, rushed him over to the tree, and ordered him to help me cut it down. Zombie-like, he complied. The saw buckled and snagged, twanged, got stuck. Smoke stung our eyes, we coughed, choked. Mel sagged a half dozen times, complaining that his heart had stopped. On each occasion I screamed hysterically, ordering him upright: so what if he croaked? I was damned if I would be responsible for the fire that set back tract housing on Long Island by two years just because I'd had the ill fortune to wind up in the Chiricahuas at 2 a.m. with a crippled ex-carnival rassler trying to expire on me!

It happened. The tree squeaked, groaned, swayed, started leaning downhill, and then, sparks flying, it crashed to the earth — as did my partner.

This time he was out cold.

Immediately, fire began spreading from the tree trunk into surrounding brush. Suddenly, I realized the blaze was much more likely to get out of hand now than when it had been confined to the erect tree. Grabbing the shovel and a kortick, I went wild for the rest of the night, circling the enor-

Autumn, near La Madera, Rio Arriba County

Grasses, Lower Ranchitos

mous pine, chopping at shrubs and brambles and little oak bushes, banging at burning leaves, plummeting uphill and down like a berserk monkey, whacking at each new outburst of flame, shoveling dirt against the trunk in a useless effort to extinguish the flames.

Two hours after dawn, Mel Marcy opened one eye and laconically observed my ministrations. After several minutes he maneuvered into an upright position and casually drawled, "Lemme have that kortick, kid, and I'll show you how it's done." I gave Mel the instrument and, astonished, watched him clear a line around the tree in five minutes.

"Now we just sit tight munching on our C rations and soaking up all this lovely sunshine while that little old fire over there just burns itself out," he said gently, leaving me with my jaw on the forest floor as he located a comfortable spot and started snoring again.

Dejectedly, I opened a ration can, discovering inside a piece of shriveled cake the size and consistency of a large pea. My feet ached; my beautiful mule-ear boots were ruined — the toes had fallen apart; *my* toes, quite literally, were exposed.

But brother, did I have a *story!*

The summer was like that, one four-star adventure after another. No sooner had I returned to the Research Station and logged a ten-hour sleep than I was off on a week-long fire below Sentinel Lookout, hiking by night into the fire, a miner's lamp hat perched on my head, in company with as strange and fascinating a group of men as I'd ever met. The straw boss, Jim West, was an ex-rodeo rider in his late twenties: he had a bullet-hole scar in one knee, a real limp because of a metal hip, and he had busted every other bone in his body at least once. A one-legged ranger called Dick hailed from Rucker Lookout. Dave Lee, a plump, sweat-drenched alcoholic from Sentinel Lookout, claimed he was wanted for income-tax evasion. A one-armed Chicano named Pete (a tank had run over him in the Korean War) had just left his wife and two kids. Little Joe couldn't stop talking about the beer and putas of Agua Prieta, the Mexican border town opposite Douglas, Arizona. Frank was a tall, taciturn, and gentle Mejicano illegally

in the U. S. A. Cardboard shoes belonging to a fifteen-year-old Rodeo kid named Johnny Johnson fell apart on the hike in, confining him to our campsite for the duration. A chunky, addle-headed old stand-up comedian called Turkey had an English vocabulary consisting of: "Got no mama, no papa, no sister, no brother, just Turkey and self . . . and wine, goddam motherfucker!" A fast-talking, jive desert corner boy had a girl's name — Isabel. A nineteen-year-old six-foot-five Anglo named Doug lugged around an enormous chain saw cutting down snags. Other assorted support personnel included the Fish and Game boys, Jerry Day and Joe Welsh (who spent most of their non-fire-fighting time tramping around the Chiricahuas thinning out mule-deer herds with their .30-.30s so the rest of the animals wouldn't starve), and Jim Strickland, a government packer, who brought in enough potatoes and fresh-killed beefsteaks to feed a small army. Finally, somebody named Jackson piloted a plane over the fire, dropped us a radio about a mile from where we had put out a parachute silk marker, then cracked up on his way home to Bisbee (or maybe it was Willcox), Arizona.

Naturally, the straw boss was prejudiced, so right away, after making camp on a windy saddle above the thirty-acre fire, we had a mini race war going. The Spanish-surnamed people settled on the south side of camp. Jim West and Johnny Johnson arranged their pine boughs north of the fire. I located about midway between the two parties because I was damned if a gimp-legged son of a bitch wearing pure-white three-hundred-dollar cowboy boots with gold stitching in the toes was going to keep me from fraternizing with just about the most intriguing bunch of people I had ever met. All during the week of fighting that lethargic blaze, it was understood that if Jim West didn't sleep with one eye open he was liable to get the rake side of a kortick embedded in his forehead, or have a handful of scorpions shoveled into his government-issue paper sleeping bag.

Those paper sleeping bags were the most phenomenal invention I'd ever laid eyes on, bar none. Problem was, however, that the Forest Service had been able to drum up only half as many bags as were needed, so we had to double up at night. I was paired with the giant snag cutter, Doug, who punched his feet through the bottom of the bag, and, given the marble-sized hail that fell that night, I almost froze to death!

We commenced fighting the brush fire by lazing around atop the ridge for a day, smoking cigarettes and bullshitting about high times in Agua Prieta, while the fire spread, doubling its size. Taking that much longer to put it out, we would be paid that much more money for our efforts. After a reasonable delay, then, we set to work, laconically scraping firewalls, keeping the blaze contained, chopping fire from the trees Doug felled, and dodging scorpions. Hundreds of the lethal insects scurried ahead of us, fleeing the flames. And once, during supper, Turkey suddenly hissed — "No te muevas!" — and slapped his broad hand hard against my thigh, killing a scorpion headed toward my crotch.

On the third day, I was working near a stand of pine trees not much taller than myself. Suddenly, one after the other, they exploded into flames like firecrackers, and I had to retreat, fast. The next day, in a drenching rain that seemed only to make the fire burn faster, I worked hard, chopping and scraping with a kortick: nearby Joe and Isabel and one-armed Pete and Frank kept up a funky chatter in English or Spanish, joking and laughing and making raunchy philosophical observations on such topics as forest fires, female anatomy, and booze, as we all methodically clambered through the smoke, half choking to death, scrabbling, cutting, and cursing. The attitude and the emotional style of my new friends thrilled me. We paused often, passing around cigarettes, like as not watching the fire jump our line and gobble up another acre, too tired for the moment to give a damn. Constantly, thunder rumbled overhead. Doug's chain saw never quit for a moment: the ripping sound of giant pines falling punctuated the forest gloom. Smoked like good hams and sausages, we turned dark gray-brown: our lips were chapped and bleeding. Yet I felt so macho and *good*, tugging on a Camel and telling Isabel to go screw himself in Spanish — "Tomalo, puto!" — every time he caught me whimpering over my blisters and called me a candy-assed gringo ... I felt so good with those people I figured I might never return to the East and re-enter that prep school full of Lord Fauntleroys and Percy Dovetonsil rich kids being programmed to commit cultural and economic genocide against Third World people like my friends here. I might just take all my money from this fire-fighting gig and rent me a room in the Rodeo motel and go down to Agua Prieta every now and then, and become a Spanish-speaking, deer-hunting, fire-fighting, guitar-picking, switchblade-carrying, pickup-driving, all-American rodeo cowboy *hero!*

I returned East, of course. But not before an additional thousand and one adventures occurred. I dug a cesspool, broke quarry rock to build a new unit at the station, mixed cement, and built a roof. I also worked for the various resident scientists, helping to collect lizards, beetles, snakes. In the evening, toward the end of dusk, we drove down to the flats between Portal and Rodeo and, with one of us seated on the front hood, spotted and captured snakes that had crawled onto the tarmac for warmth. Or we searched shale slides for rock rattlers up in the hills. I caught large iridescent green gloriosa beetles for an entomologist called Smythe, and hunted mites in the desert for another man. I fought a last fire up around Sally Falls, just me and Jim West, both of us on horseback. I killed a four-foot-long black-tailed rattlesnake — the first and last rattler I ever killed — skinned it and made a belt. Riding home after two days on that fire, we turned a trail corner and reined in, startled as hell. Before us, in a wide area that had been burned over last year, the grass was waist high, and so green it resembled the sea. A hundred charred spikes of burnt-out pines rose from the grass at regular intervals. And over fifty mule deer, flashing their white hind ends, bounded rabbit-like away from us, the kind of opulent, wild sight I doubt I'll ever see again.

I capped off the summer by hitting Agua Prieta accompanied by some of the guys with whom I'd fought forest fires: Pedro and Tarzan, Felipe and Frank. We attended a sham bullfight, got drunk, and went to the Vista, the red-light district. I was too scared to get laid, but I drank plenty of beer and punched coins into jukeboxes as we traveled from one bar to another and my friends kept requesting keys from the bartender and going in back with the girls. About 3 a.m. we finally headed for Rodeo in an old pickup with one-armed Pete at the wheel and the rest of us tumbled in back, vomiting and singing and moaning. Me, I just lay there stupefied, a lot drunker than I'd ever been, feeling as sweet and as dumb and as crazy as if I were at the very mysterious Heart of Life that few people out-

Camposanto, Taos Valley

Las Colonias Valley

side of my friends here had ever discovered. Staring up at the rarefied universe while the tires hummed, I could not force the mariachi music from my head. Although dizzy and giggly, I also felt as if I were living a legend or a myth, partaking of something wonderful in human experience that rarely occurred, and would last far beyond my normal lifetime.

Later on, back East, I guess I pumped up the memory of that western experience as much as I dared. Yet I never forgot how it had really been. I never forgot what a windmill on the flats is like, or how I was enraptured by the soft patterns of that valley beneath Justin Locke's Taos adobe. The abundance of hummingbirds in Portal stayed with me; as did the way it was to chop with a kortick on a steep hillside among men moving like ghosts through thick smoke and the rain, calling to each other in Spanish. I never forgot the wideness and suddenness of weather in that country; nor disremembered the danger and anticipation of moving gingerly through a landscape where rattlesnakes lived. I never forgot the impossibly high grass in that burnt-out forest, and the pack of mule deer bounding away like rabbits. And I never forgot the people, or the way they fit into that landscape: cowboys, forest rangers, braceros.

And that lone buzzard, circling a mile high. And the white cattle skull glittering in the sand. And the little lizards. And Rodeo, New Mexico, with its fallen trees and the empty railroad trestle, its windmills and crumbling adobe houses, and cottonwood fluff falling like snow in the hundred-degree heat, gathering in drifts on the highway bisecting town. Gathering until a lone car, let's call it an old Cadillac convertible, comes speeding through town at a hundred miles an hour with the radio blasting a Kitty Wells tune, making all that white fluff boil up in its wake so that long after its passing the soft cottonwood snow is settling back to earth, surreal, beautiful, lonely as hell —

Out West.

Eleven years later I returned to that country, strung out, on edge, going down fast, and scared stiff.

Looking back, I think 1968, a bad year for everyone, was the roughest year of my life. It was the year of the big garbage strike in New York and of the Tet Offensive in Vietnam. Emotionally drained, politically unstable, I paced the New York streets, passing between stacks of garbage sometimes up to my shoulder. Icy winter wind splashed newspapers with shrill war headlines and pictures of unimaginable slaughter against my legs. After three years of concentrated anti-war activity, I thought: This is it, this is when the Vietnamese finally win, they are at last going to push us out of there, and it will be over and I can breathe again. I couldn't believe it when the Tet Offensive did not end that war, letting me off the hook. Impossible to believe it also when Martin Luther King and then Bobby Kennedy were assassinated. Later on, the Chicago Democratic Convention landed a haymaker to my so-called radic-lib chin. Involved in it all, I had become a useless person. I had so much rage against the U. S. Military, the U. S. Government, U. S. History, my own blindered upbringing, and all the sociology nobody had ever taught me in college, that I could barely function. My novels had disintegrated into shrill, polemical, nihilistic tracts.

One story I began that year gave me reason to revisit my old western haunts. It concerned a relationship between a middle-class New England Wasp and his old prep school friend, a western Indian who had developed into a major-league-caliber baseball pitcher, winning the Rookie of the Year award his first season up. Then, called to Vietnam, the pitcher suffered a shrapnel wound in his right shoulder. My book opened during spring training with the pitcher attempting a comeback after his war experience. His old Wasp friend, now a newspaper reporter, had been sent South to cover the story. There was no story, however: the pitcher had lost his stuff. Eventually, he and the reporter wound up on a cross-country odyssey, heading for the pitcher's home reservation, where thousands of sheep had just been chemicaled into oblivion in a mishap reminiscent of an animal kill that occurred some years before at the Dugway Proving Grounds in Utah.

My brief southwestern journey, then, took place under the guise of gathering material, checking out landscape and landmarks, and in general reacquainting myself with the territory in which my characters would act out their drama.

More truthfully, I don't really know why I went. I was scared, nervous, uptight. I thought if I had to spend another minute in the guerrilla-warfare tension of New York City, I would either commit suicide or hit the streets with an indiscriminately blazing rifle. So to save my soul and my ass, I did what we Yankee North Americans always ineffectually do, and jumped into a moving vehicle. I hit the road, looking for solace in motion, searching for answers and a little peace through travel and a change of scene — one of the most overrated and underproductive panaceas ever to come down the Great American Pike.

Departing New York on the day Martin Luther King was assassinated, I took a bus straight to Colorado Springs, where I rented a VW beetle and hit the road, heading south, doing four, five, six hundred miles a day. Driving along, I made notes on what caught my eye. Trees in dry stream beds were like frozen hag's hair. Car hulls were sunk into the sand. On the radio, in between news programs featuring the riots prompted by King's death, evangelists were having a heyday. A preacher told me that "a tumult worse than the tumult of war was the tumult and heat of the sinful heart." And he prayed that the Communists would fear us because *we* stand for freedom.

All along the road, lining the shoulders, were reddish-brown beer bottles. They glinted from out of the dry furze, bright shots of sunlight popping off them, one right after another, down the line like a kind of solar machine-gunning, hurting my eyes.

Moving into New Mexico, I passed corrugated-tin and tar-paper shacks. Cars were stacked in dusty corrals, "as if once they'd been horses, or people had hoped they were horses." Later on I wrote, "There seems to be a real ill treatment of cars, a kind of resentment in the way they lie in the arroyos and washes, so totally deserted."

The radio said that a white man had been dragged from his automobile in Cincinnati and stabbed to death.

I kept moving, past a ghost town, a quick image of old wooden buildings, broken and bullet-holed glass, collapsed corral fences. In Taos, I remarked on an Indian, wrapped in a blanket, whom a hippie girl was kissing. In a blink, I was gone, ripping along in the wash of a Coors beer truck. Come dark I passed a huge drive-in movie screen showing the final moments of *Bonnie and Clyde*. And an enormous tumbleweed loping straight toward the car gave me such a fright I almost swerved hard enough to tip over.

When the sun dawned, it glinted off HELP IMPEACH EARL WARREN signs. A radio editorial criticized Ramsey Clark for being more concerned about rioters' lives than property. Editorials in the papers I bought, and on the car radio, seemed unanimously in favor of shooting looters. I gave up hope for humankind.

Buzzards and ravens leaped off jackrabbit carcasses as I bore down on them. Ronald Reagan wanted us to use military force to retrieve the *Pueblo* from North Korea. Sparrow hawks perched on telephone lines gazed quietly into oily green mesquite. The sagebrush was aluminum green. A big tumbleweed about a quarter mile off the road spun around high in the air, caught in the funnel of a dust devil.

Stopping at a Lota Burger, I listened as the radio described Operation Complete Victory. The goal was to "eliminate the enemy" from around Saigon. A father led his son from a neighboring car toward the bathroom. The kid's sweat shirt said, "How can we lose when we're so sincere?"

Rodeo, New Mexico, was just another crummy desert heap with a lot of paper and plastic garbage hung up in dead bushes, and discarded cans and broken bottles everywhere, and a few chickens and dogs wandering among the car hulls. A discarded yellow truck had bullet holes in the windshield. A railroad dining car, once a café, was now a private home. A smoking stovepipe tilted out of the roof; windows were boarded over. I wrote, "Weeds in all yards. Just a mess of greasy junk. Huge hunks of rusted machinery on both sides of the road. Hamm's beer."

At the Southwestern Research Station beyond Portal dozens of hummingbirds all sizes and all colors of the rainbow abounded. But I was nervous, straining at some bit, impatient to move on. Next morning I stopped at the Geronimo Surrender monument south of Rodeo in a place — no town, no nothing — called Apache. The air was absolutely silent; it sizzled without noise. The monument is a stone phallus about fifteen feet high in a roadside rest area. Behind it is a little stone latrine and two picnic tables under a thatch sunshade. Yucca plants, barbed wire . . . and a thick carpet of yellow flowers growing around the base of nearby soft hills. I heard a mourning dove coo. And remembered how Miles and Gatewood had promised Geronimo and Nachite one thing, then delivered another, shipping their people to Florida, where the strange land and the damp weather killed them.

Storm over Taos Mountain

Moon over Carson Mesa, west of Taos

On the other side of the Chiricahuas, I stopped in San Carlos, an Apache reservation dotted with small green and yellow houses. Women wore long-sleeved blouses and ankle-length dresses. At the end of San Carlos Avenue, a United States jet trainer was on display. The bizarre sight left me speechless. Maybe it was just a reminder, so the Apache people would never get it into their heads to try another ghost dance, or whatever their equivalent of that ritual might be.

Show Low, Snowflake, I was *moving*. The enormous grassy flatness of Navajo country kept me real quiet. Wideness, desolation, solitude, incredible beauty, poverty. Open range — no fences. I picked up a man who had been waiting all night for a ride: destination? — "White Cone." He had a scarred face, folded his arms, kept still. As we passed some mangy-looking horses, he made his only comment in fifty miles: "Them's skinny horses." He said it with a chagrined, deprecating smile. Then he nodded to be let off, and I braked: he headed straight into the enormous emptiness and disappeared.

On the Hopi Second Mesa, I zoomed past squat rock buildings with black peepholes, and a few aluminum Quonset huts. A scarecrow seemed ludicrous in a patch of bedraggled cornstalks growing from sheer sand in the middle of a waterless desert. Big, broad-shouldered girder giants carried looping electric lines westward from power plants in Farmington. I felt insignificant, that's for sure. Also beleaguered by the colors of bleached-out burnt umber. Then I passed piles of enormous red boulders. In the Painted Desert huge gray-green piles of rock and sand resembled melted elephants. The hills squirmed in the heat. Big plops of rusty rock, molded sandstone — they looked like huge cowflops. Other enormous boulders lay in a frozen jumble at the foot of vermilion cliffs.

I sped up into the Kaibab Forest, stopping briefly to eat a sandwich: the wind roared in tall pines with an ocean-like sound. Beyond Zion National Park, I hit a snowstorm that turned out to be floating peach blossoms. A dust storm and drifting sand made the trip into Las Vegas trying.

One night I spent there, and got out. Heading back toward Colorado Springs, I thought a good title for my new novel might be *The Man with a Coonskin Heart*. In Hanksville, Utah, the rest-room toilet bowl was clogged with shit. Cow tracks marked the sand dunes. At night, the alkali in road dips where little flash floods had deposited it was fluorescent. I crossed the Rockies at night, under a full moon, breathing air heavy with dust and juniper. Back in Colorado Springs, exhausted, I couldn't go to sleep because I could hear my heart beating loudly: it seemed to echo in the springs of the mattress, and I was frightened.

I had traveled close to three thousand miles in five days.

And that book about the baseball pitcher and the newspaper reporter never got written.

That autumn at my alma mater, Hamilton College, my wife and I watched the filming of my first novel, *The Sterile Cuckoo*. I loved the director, Alan Pakula, and all the people involved with the film. But at the same time I was embarrassed by all the money being spent for what seemed then like such a trite thing. I could barely stay civil. How could I justify all that hullabaloo over so little when our B-52s were incinerating so many people per second in an imperialist race war? When I talked economics with a former professor and good friend, I was boggled by his conservative and indifferent approach to it all.

I could not talk to people without getting angry and proselytizing. I accused them of moral atrophy if I found them politically ignorant. Also I could not bear the implications of all that I was learning. I didn't want to lose my love of America or of the way of life that had carried me so successfully through my first twenty-five years. I was terrified of being forced to become a militant radical thanks to political understandings I now possessed.

Ruby and I talked about leaving New York, moving somewhere. Logically, New England is where we should have gone. Most members of our peer group who couldn't take it any more seemed headed for little farms in quaint Vermont towns. But we had no desire to run away to a safe hiding place. More important to remain politically active and involved. After all, who wanted to retire at thirty? And if you live in the heart of the belly of the monster, why abdicate by slinking off to some semi-alcoholic rural euphoria among the New Yorkified middle class? Last but never least, why follow over the grass trampled flat by all the other lemmings?

About the Southwest I had my memories and stories. It

was a place neither of us had ever lived in or even visited at length. Still, we knew a little about Taos and something about New Mexico. We knew about Reies Tijerina and his land-grant movement in the North. We understood people were very poor, and their situation was becoming highly politicized and publicized.

For a while, I had been reading a radical Chicano movement newspaper, *El Grito del Norte.* Though it was published in Española, an hour south of Taos, it was possible to buy copies in New York. From the paper we had learned much about the history and current problems of the North. We knew that Rio Arriba, Taos, and Mora counties, which comprise the central land area of the North, were among the poorest counties in the nation. They compared to places in Mississippi and areas like Beaufort County, South Carolina. More than half the Spanish-speaking families in that part of New Mexico earned less than $3,000 a year; well over half the inhabitants received some sort of welfare. The per capita income was around $1,200: it was $3,800 nationwide. Official unemployment in Rio Arriba County often rose as high as 25 percent; in Taos County, 15 percent; in Mora County, 40 percent. During the tourist season those statistics shrunk, but most of the jobs available were low-paying service jobs at a dollar to a dollar eighty an hour, wages that simply reinforced a poverty culture.

Too, because of racist, monolingual school policies, the Hispanic people averaged only 7.1 years of schooling (as opposed to 9.0 nationwide for blacks, and 12.1 for Anglos). Chicanos twenty-five or older averaged only five years of schooling: Taos High School was not so humorously dubbed a "prep school for the Army."

For years, an ugly land battle had been taking place there. From the time the Treaty of Guadalupe Hidalgo was signed, ending the U.S. invasion of Mexico in 1848, and guaranteeing the protection of Hispanic ejido lands, it had been repeatedly violated. In 1854 Congress passed laws declaring communal lands to be public domain, and in 1906 Teddy Roosevelt incorporated much of that land into national forests. A new legal system, carried on in a language people did not understand, had been working overtime to separate indigenous people from their holdings. An incomprehensible tax system had aided the process. To hold on to land people had to pay for surveys and legal expenses, but they had no cash. Lawyers,

known as black vultures, became rich taking payment in land for fighting land battles. Infamous groups, like the Catron-Elkin ring of Santa Fe, acquired millions of private and communally held lands during the late 1800s. A U.S. Court of Private Land Claims set up in 1891, composed solely of Anglos, further abetted the robbery.

The Forest Service now owned 44 percent of Taos County, land which prior to 1906 had been communally owned, and had been the mainstay of an agricultural subsistence farming and ranching economy. During the past fifteen years grazing permits on Forest Service land in the North had been reduced by 50 to 60 percent, driving all but the hardiest local small ranchers out of business. Why? In order to manage the forests primarily for mining, timbering, tourist, recreation, and retirement interests.

Only two years earlier, on June 5, 1967, bitterness over northern New Mexico's land situation had exploded into the famous courthouse "raid" in Tierra Amarilla, two hours directly west of Taos, when a citizen's arrest of a local district attorney, by Reies Tijerina–led land-grant members, had flared into a violent encounter publicized around the world. The apprehension of the D. A., Alfonso Sánchez, had been planned in retaliation for much police repression of local land-grant heirs who for some years, as members of Tijerina's Alianza Federal de Mercedes (Land Grant Alliance), had been struggling to achieve a return of their stolen lands. The arrest went awry, however: a state cop and a jailer were wounded; a deputy sheriff and a newspaper reporter were briefly kidnapped; and many land-grant heirs who had approached the courthouse intending to carry out a legal action wound up fleeing into the surrounding mountains and remote villages. State authorities were so shaken they sent the National Guard into Tierra Amarilla, Canjilon, and other small towns of that area; even several tanks made an appearance. And a Gestapo-like roundup and intensified repression of local residents took place.

No question about it, we would be moving into a hornet's nest. The myth of Taos as a community where three cultures lived together in perfect harmony was just that — a Chamber of Commerce – inspired snow job.

Complicating matters further, northern New Mexico had recently been chosen for a kind of freak mecca. Thousands of

One view from Lower Ranchitos

Looking across mesa toward Arroyo Seco

hippies from the East and West coasts were moving into the impoverished northern counties, buying up land individually or starting communes, further inflaming the passions of a long-oppressed people, and adding to the general frustrating confusion that often prevails in our country.

To justify living in Taos, we hoped that our political awareness would locate us on the correct side of the class struggle going down in the North.

In May 1969, almost two years after the Tierra Amarilla courthouse raid, I drove into Taos with an eight-thousand-dollar check from the Literary Guild in my pocket, parked my suitcase at the El Chico Motor Court, and began looking for a house to rent or buy.

I had not traveled a hundred yards before I almost ran into a brand-new Mustang with DESTROY THE HIPPIES adhesive-taped along its right side. A few minutes later I sat down in Spivey's Café for breakfast, looked up, and noticed a sign tacked on the wall in front of me: HELP KEEP AMERICA BEAUTIFUL, TAKE A HIPPY TO A CARWASH. Other signs around town proclaimed belligerently: WE RESERVE THE RIGHT TO REFUSE SERVICE TO ANYONE WE CONSIDER A HEALTH HAZARD.

The quaint little Taos Plaza seemed like a spin-off of New York City. Dozens of longhairs wrapped in cheap Pendleton blankets were pretending to be Indians and asking for handouts and looking for peyote meetings. Teeny-B groupie types with tatoozies on their foreheads accompanied them: the whole schmeer — New York Southwest . . . the Little Big Manzana.

Entering the first real estate office in my path, I asked to be shown around. As we puttered about in her decrepit VW, the agent informed me, "That's Horse Thief Shorty's corner we're passing right now. Somebody fired six shots into a microbus here last night, but nobody was hurt." And: "That there is Joe Sage's Macrobiotic Restaurant. The reason the front window's all taped up is somebody threw a brick through the plate glass last night."

Back in the El Chico Motor Court that night, it took me a while to fall asleep. Much of what I thought about was echoed in an *El Grito* article published three months later, on July 9, 1969. Addressing hippies, the paper said:

> Think about the fact that, much as you reject your middle-class Anglo society and its values, you are still seen here as gringos. Anglos. Think about the 120-year-old struggle by chicanos and the even older struggle by Indians to get back millions of acres of land stolen from them by Anglo ranchers with their Anglo lawyer buddies. Think about what it means for a new influx of Anglos — no matter how different their purpose from those others — to come in and buy up land that the local people feel to be theirs and cannot afford to buy themselves. Think about the fact that a real estate agent in Taos reports having sold almost $500,000 worth of land to longhairs . . . .

> Think about this: the longhair has opted out. Most of the chicanos and Indians have no option — except revolution. People here cannot flee to islands of peace in a nation of horrors, this *is* their nation. It cannot be said too often: there is a long, hard political and economic struggle in these beautiful mountains, a struggle for land and justice. That struggle calls for fighters and supporters, not refugees with their own set of problems. You may see the scenery as relief from an oppressive America; we see a battleground against oppression.

Next day, Sunday, I hit town early. Cruising slowly along the main drag, I noticed a disquieting scene taking place near Cantu's Furniture and Hardware Store. A tall blond freak, seated under the portal, looked very uncomfortable. Across the street, right beside a hippie General Store with a broken front window, a local man stared malevolently across the road at the hippie. South of the portal, another local man, his eyes narrowed menacingly, seemed to be slowly stalking the blond kid. Just north of the portal, a third local man appeared to be inching toward the freak, real hostility in his barely perceptible gait. I veered over, opened the passenger door, and asked, "Can I give you a ride anywhere?"

Tumbling in, he slammed the door, and blurted, "Wow, mister, am I glad to see you! Let's get out of here!"

"What's going on?"

"Damned if I know. I was just waiting around, man,

y'know? To see if the General Store was gonna open. When those three guys showed up — "

He lived about ten miles southeast of town near the small Llano Quemado community where my friend Justin Locke had his house, in the Five Star Farm commune, located across an arroyo from the Ponce de Leon Hot Springs at the base of the Sangre de Cristo foothills.

Less than twenty-four hours after my arrival in Taos, I suddenly found myself lying naked in the midday sun beside an old-fashioned concrete mineral pool, surrounded by pleasantly naked men and women, most of them young and a little glassy-eyed from various drugs. Over by another hippie shack, a bearded guy chopped wood. From across the arroyo drifted thick aromas arising from a big cauldron in which the Five Star Farm's supper was cooking.

Sun-warmed, I grew drowsy. I couldn't believe it. A sexy-looking woman from Florida settled beside me: we started talking, and pretty soon she said, "You and I should make it together tonight." Opening one eye, I shook my head and drifted off again. *Where had I been all my life?*

The idyll collapsed moments later when a carload of local men parked above the springs, debouched, and popped open beers. Their presence changed everything. Women and most men got dressed; a few freaks drifted into the nearby shack where they had enough guns and ammunition to defend a dozen Alamos. While everybody became nervous, the guy chopping wood put the ax through his foot, and a party rushed him off to the hospital. The blond kid I had picked up in town led me across the arroyo to the Five Star Farm, explaining as he went that the Chicanos were going to attack that night, which is why they had stockpiled an arsenal. But I should stick around for supper, spend the night, I might really have some fun. Besides, he thought that chick I had been talking to really liked me and we would have a good time together.

Dinner I could handle. But, declining the invitation to spend the night and participate in their race war, I slunk home afterward, amazed, as always, at how skillfully the system can divide and conquer.

At week's end, Ruby flew out, and we went over all the houses I had looked at. Aware of the local dicho, "He who sells his land sells his mother," we did not want to buy from long-time local folks. Too much bitterness accompanied their selling. As much as possible, we wished to avoid supporting the process by which Spanish-speaking people were losing, or being forced to sell, their land.

In the end, we bought the cheapest house available, a $14,500 five-room adobe on 1.7 acres approximately a mile west of the Taos Plaza in a small community called Upper Ranchitos. Because the Anglo telephone lineman who owned it had a bunch of mortgages going, the down payment for this choice piece of real estate turned out to be exactly everything I had in my pocket, namely eight grand.

But we had done it. We both felt queasy, apprehensive. That house was my first debt ever; I felt sick at heart.

Yet magpies cavorted in the cottonwood trees, arrogantly chattering. Redwing blackbirds and meadowlarks populated the pasture next door. And, walking into our little back field for the first time, suddenly there was Taos Mountain.

I can't recall how it looked to me then. Ownership of land gave me no thrill, only apprehension. An awareness of the political, economic, and social situation in Taos did nothing but increase the guilt I felt at being able to afford the property. I worried that our politics could not counteract the energy of our simple middle-class presence, and we would add to the dislocating process tormenting the Taos Valley.

The mortgage debt was bad. Too, the simple legal responsibilities of ownership could make me feel faint. Suppose some neighbor's kid should fall in the front irrigation ditch and drowned — I could be sued, maybe held criminally negligible. Now I had property taxes and insurance to pay; I would have to make contributions to volunteer fire departments. Upkeep and repair — who can imagine what those costs would be? Suppose a cottonwood fell onto the house in a gale. Or squashed the car? Or the *kid?* What if we hated it here?

Vey iz mir!

Still, I enjoy thinking I forgot all that for a moment while gazing at the mountain from my future home within its sphere of influence. I know it was a sunny late afternoon; snow tarried yet around the summits. No doubt a couple of enormous ravens floated slowly by, croaking softly. From the neighboring pasture a few cows laconically gave us the once-over. Noises carried over from the grammar school playground a mile away, kids playing baseball. Upper Ranchitos Road was un-

If these mountains die, where will our imaginations wander?

Walking rain near Tres Orejas Mountain

paved back then: a faint beige mist hung over fields from the passage of cars all day long. And nighthawks overhead chased insects, beeping methodically.

So there we were, owners of property.

All my political, anti-capitalist propaganda to the contrary.

Leaping into the VW bus, we drove it nonstop, forty-four hours, back to New York City, packed up our belongings and, in July, left for good.

Somewhere in West Virginia, on the midnight between July 22 and 23, the VW bus pulled onto a shoulder, and I veered our U-Haul van in behind it. Ruby swung out holding a cupcake in which a single tiny candle burned. Handing it to me under the summertime full moon, she sang "Happy Birthday."

I had just turned twenty-nine.

In Kansas, fat pheasants lined the route, so many it almost seemed as if we were passing in military review. Then we climbed over La Veta Pass, which separates Walsenburg, Colorado, from Fort Garland. Asters beside the road floated like a radiant mauve mist. Aspen forests trembled like the rippling of green sunshine on quiet water. Although I have negotiated La Veta a hundred times since, never has it been as clear and as right as when we drove over back then, bringing all our earthly goods to Taos. Beyond Fort Garland we traveled through flat farming country and sagebrush plains. Tractors plied the potato and lettuce fields; the Sangre de Cristos extended south on our left; more soft hills arose again thirty miles westward, across the Rio Grande Gorge. Horned larks and turquoise-colored mountain bluebirds scattered in sprightly bunches as we whizzed along.

Lord, you really *could* see forever!

South of San Luis, Colorado, flights of ducks populated a sewage lagoon — goldeneyes, ruddy ducks, coots, buffleheads; and a big flock of sharp-winged nighthawks dipsy-doodled dangerously over the macadam, chasing insects. Then the sagebrush turned a golden-green-mauve color seemingly imbued with a lucid fluorescence: it was the rainy season.

Roller-coaster curves and hills began at Questa, an hour north of Taos. Momentum carried us through the green picture-book valleys of San Cristobal and Arroyo Hondo. Then the road leveled out, making its final run into Taos.

Facing south from the mesa above Arroyo Hondo, the Taos Valley is ten miles away; the Cinemascope panorama must encompass thousands of square miles. Cottonwood veins against the mountains delineate streams descending from hidden wilderness lakes: the Arroyo Seco Creek, the Rio Lucero, the Pueblo River, the Rio Fernando de Taos, and, way south in the Ranchos-Talpa Valley, Pot Creek, the Rio Chiquito, and the Little Rio Grande. Those last three join into a single river that flows westward about ten miles through Llano Quemado, Talpa, Ranchos de Taos, and Cordillera, meeting the Pueblo River in Los Córdovas. Then it descends through a gorge until finally reaching the Rio Grande. You can see Vallecitos and Wheeler peaks, and the back of Taos Mountain. Beyond Llano Quemado, thirty miles away, rises the entirely wooded mountain called Picuris Peak. Behind it and to the east is the bald Jicarita Peak, and the wild-looking — snow-streaked even in July — Truchas Peak. To the southwest a hundred miles away stands a small flat-topped mountain called Pedernal in Abiquiu, home of the famous artist Georgia O'Keeffe. Closer to Taos, near the one-post-office, five-ruin community of Carson west of the Rio Grande, is Tres Orejas Peak. Across the sagebrush plain and piñon forest, almost due west now, are mountains rising above Tierra Amarilla and Canjilon and other tiny mountain villages. More to the north is the upside-down bowl of San Antonio Mountain, where the elk and the antelope are —

But we didn't know the names back then. We simply confronted the majestic scenery with apprehension and a bit of awe, pushing our vehicles past lush pastureland dotted by grazing cows and horses . . . and wound up trapped in our first traffic jam since Manhattan three miles north of Taos in El Prado!

Abruptly, it was a hundred degrees out. The air, clogged with construction dust, instantly made our kid, Luke, cranky. Our cats complained loudly, pissing all over our earthly possessions. It took almost an hour to drive the final two miles home!

They were fixing the roads.

In Taos, they are always fixing the roads in summertime.

This activity is always planned to coincide with the height of the tourist season in order to inconvenience as many people as possible. There is only one road bisecting Taos north and south. In those days it was a two-lane ribbon of potholed, frost-heaved, diabolically unshouldered macadam. At the center of town, a single stoplight marshaled the entire traffic flow arriving or wishing to depart.

After an epic and exciting odyssey into the realm of our New Lives, we arrived at the house cranky, sweat-soaked, and dust-covered thanks to the herculean task of traversing that final mile.

In September of that year, I returned to New York — to pick up the last of our things, make some money lecturing at Franklin and Marshall, and attend a private screening of *The Sterile Cuckoo.* But while uptown helping to get out a fund-raising mailing for a cooperative clinic in Tierra Amarilla, New Mexico, I loaned my car to a fellow worker who hit a child in the heart of Harlem. And my eastern trip became a nightmare. The incident closed out my New York life.

Driving west after that disastrous sojourn, I spent a night whimpering through fantastic thunder-and-lightning storms in Kansas. The heavens shattered: sheet lightning exploded so constantly I had no need of headlights. I drove for miles in a spectacular downpour, the entire landscape ghastly bright with terrifying and grotesque electrical fluorescence. For certain I believed I would be crushed by boulders of thunder, or by its shock waves. Flash floods seemed imminent. How could I not be hit, electrocuted, or fried to a crisp? I shouted from fright, wanting to stop; but was afraid to halt, and pushed on.

Somewhere on the western plains the weather abated. Come morning, snow powdered thousands of acres of corn stubble; and shallow rain lakes miles wide were covered by flotillas of migrating ducks. In eastern Colorado hay bales, white on one side, dotted wide fields like gigantic sugar cubes. The plow tracks of recently worked fields were finely traced in white. Then there were acres of winter wheat, the plants bright green, the ground between rows pure white.

Parking the car, I got out, embracing that vast landscape, grateful for whatever it had been that had launched me into an existence west of the Mississippi.

A few miles east of Fort Garland, I found a dead great horned owl beside the road, and put it in the car. With almost slavish gratitude for the magpies, and Taos Mountain, and tiny fields pocked with hay bales, I reached Taos. The aspens and cottonwoods were turning yellow. When I raised my hand in greeting to a car driven by a stranger and received a salutation in return, I knew I had arrived at a place worth trying to call home.

And it was time to settle in.

Rainbow, Cerros de Taos

Part IV

LAND, MOODS, WEATHER

She lives on the mesa where the road rises out of the Rio Grande Gorge and confronts for the first time that panorama of the entire valley and the high plain: the mountains, Taos and all its satellite villages and rivers, the Rio Grande Gorge, the forests and the mountains to the west and to the far north. Her house has no running water, but it has large windows and sunshine. It is surrounded by sagebrush, a few junipers, some piñon trees. White bones for her dogs are scattered around the front stoop. In a twisted tree by the door, hot breezes stir a vague wind chime. Beside the house is a rough table on which stand her sculpture pieces —they are powerful, of this earth, metal-like stones and sculptured granite, ready for flight. Her face is lined, tough, passionate. She wears dark glasses, a kerchief, gold earrings, a bright blouse, black pants, boots. Her fingernails are broken, chipped from working; she has calluses on her hands. She uses acetylene, and wears goggles, cutting and bending metal. She has a pistol, and when a rattlesnake appeared near the cold shack south of the house where she works, she took a shot at it, but missed. She smokes Mexican cigarettes and walks with powerful strides through the sagebrush, heading for the river rim a mile away. She moves strongly, preoccupied, intensely. Inside her house there is a sense of organic correctness: feathers, spider webs, little trinkets, a juniper sprig, Ché Guevara, Eugene Debs, a large painting of the sun over mighty canyon lands. I learn from her the consummate values. She is earthy, passionate, political. She calls herself cojo, manco, tuerto, drinks sherry, works very hard, loves very hard, absorbs landscape with desperate, beautiful joy, lives alone. She awakens in blue pre-dawn on the mesa and opens the door. Sunshine has illuminated the tiny triangle of the Wheeler Peak summit visible behind Taos Mountain — nothing more. Wrapped in an old red velvet robe, she drinks strong coffee and smokes a cigarette, watching me sleep. I am aware of her. Her arrogant, broken, powerful gift makes me feel more whole than I believe I will ever feel again. A great joy resides in the center of our sadness. She is so rare and special I am surprised at her love for me. A horse rears or gallops when she moves. Her big body, her work, her eyes, her political compassion, her lust for life, her desire to twist light from all the dark situations. She drives a car with a sun roof open in midwinter: ice batters her dreams. She sculpts the true forms and they gleam, at rest or taking flight. Bold, iron-like, some of them are like boulders from the gorge, so heavy in line they could kill you bluntly, so sensuous they are like bodies floating weightless and slick after lovemaking. Her energy flows from here to the skyline, and from the swift slicing pattern of a jay's shadow, and from the symbolic sweetness of a meadowlark. I want to break her bones, hurt her back, stun her for opening up this much world. She coughs but continues smoking. In the cold air, flesh steams. We wash white bodies from a porcelain saucepan, drink beer, laugh, eat tacos, play the guitar. The tragedy is that Allende is dead, the experiment over. Under the apple tree we weep for Chile, Neruda, Victor Jara. Out on the mesa, coyotes are barking, I listen to them —she is sleeping. The house smells like black tobacco. It's cold. They are hunting out there, coming closer, their calls growing louder. I get goose bumps. It seems as if they are almost at the door. Getting up, I step outside. My flesh aches, feels bruised, is scratched and slightly bleeding. My body feels immortal.

I can see all the stars in heaven.

Later, I stand in my back field, watching the grass burn. Her car pulls into the driveway. She approaches uncomfortably and hands me a copy of Moby Dick *illustrated by Rockwell Kent. I wish to ask forgiveness, and give thanks. Suddenly everything becomes too late, and my innocence can't understand fully the precious thing I am losing.*

Alone on a dark night, she listens, on her shortwave, to Radio Habana. In the morning, she discovers the shape of magpie wings lifting off the snow. I'll never forget the coyotes. She made them perfect.

I'm not saying it was all good. Or that just like that we were saved. It wasn't easy, and in the end we weren't saved. Many things fell apart as they often do. Eight years later, after a divorce, my kids come up from Albuquerque on the Trailways bus every two or three weeks; we also spend the summers together. There is always that sadness in the background. Fortunately, there is a steady love too. It exists for all of us, and is as sustaining as the blue hills.

Sometimes I add up the experiences, the traumatic ebb and flow, and I get so scared that not even the sight of a magpie landing in the dying pear tree outside the kitchen window cheers me up. Once an indestructible athlete, now I can feel the not so subtle decay of my body. I also realize how the human spirit can be pushed close to the edge under the pressure of a difficult history. Doubts remain over the wisdom of these roots I have planted. I feel bad about people I love whose absence makes me forever unwhole. I despise certain longings that corrupt my desire to sculpt political and ethical values which can have a say-so on worldly stages. I'm scared more than I'm confident, I think. I'm sick of certain struggles, can't adapt to others, and find myself caught between opposite tendencies too often for comfort. With envy I observe neighbors — a small farmer working beside me on the ditch, an old Pueblo friend who walks through his bean field humorously cursing the wild morning glory — with envy I observe them and feel bereft because I do not have the ability — I lack the emotional makeup — to accept simpler rhythms of time and place. I cannot ease down into a less pressurized landscape; I have difficulty pausing to appreciate.

A few months ago, shortly after Christmas, I attended a funeral at the Pueblo. After the church service, family and Pueblo friends accompanied the body to the graveyard within the ruins of an old church destroyed in the 1847 Pueblo Revolt. My place was outside the walls on a cold, stinging day — yet very sunny, the sky smooth, penetratingly blue. Standing outside the walls, I watched them group around the grave, everyone wrapped in colorful blankets. Their wailing reached me as tiny bursts of sound, bird-like against the looming mountain.

The day was so clear and beautiful it hurt like a thousand silver needles. For all the unhappiness involved, their gathering was a solid image. I don't think I romanticize their roots, for I understand they are as torn and as bitter as I am; in fact, many of my Pueblo friends suffer degrees of spiritual and physical abuse I have never begun to know. A historical cruelty battering their lives — their religious lives, their working lives, their banal day-to-day, flat-tire, home-loan, television, welfare, Mary Hartman lives — that cruelty battering their lives I could not begin to cope with.

Still, they have a visible and functional ritual to mark all the major turning points. And a deeply ingrained place from where to roam. Often it helps them no more than it helps me. Yet for them the earth is a real basis of struggle, and of cultural dignity and personal identity. And I am inordinately grateful to all those in the valley who have allowed me access to the mechanics of this knowledge.

Understand, I don't want to be precious about land or landscape, or about living close to the earth. My friend from Fort Thompson, South Dakota — he is Sioux — looks at me and says sarcastically and angrily: "Who gives a good goddam about the beautiful sunset? What did the beautiful sunset ever do for me? Can you eat the sunset? Can you jam a couple of .30-.30 shells into your rifle and knock down the sunset at two hundred yards, and quick-like slit its throat so all the blood will pump out and not ruin the meat, and drag it home and chop it up and throw it into a frying pan with a lot of lard and then eat it? Don't talk to me about the beautiful sunset!"

Still, land sustains. Sometimes you turn a corner and an aspen tree or the shape of a cloud will knock you flat on your ass with a quick little uppercut you never in a million years expected, and you might burst into tears. From the poetic hurt of it all.

A few years ago I could not look at a pretty hill, or at a flowering fruit tree, or at a deer in my cousin's orchard without superimposing over it an Asiafication of the same scene: yellow-skinned children fleeing naked, napalm on their backs; bloated water buffaloes, shot for fun by passing U.S. GIs, rotting in bomb-cratered rice paddies. And I would always think: *For me to enjoy this, my agents are doing that to them, to a whole lot of thems, someplace else.*

There were years when I just couldn't accept the gift of autumn maple leaves, or snow-covered bird feeders, or a walk in the spring rain without feeling terribly guilty.

Pablo Neruda once wrote about Spain:

And you will ask: Why doesn't his poetry
speak of dreams and leaves
and the great volcanoes of his native land?

Come and see the blood in the streets.
Come and see
the blood in the streets.
Come and see the blood
in the streets!

So when I become involved in a project like this I want to make sure one of its reasons for being is that nobody out there will be allowed to forget the antonyms for some of the natural beauty still going strong in the United States of America. Granted, I find it a fairly grisly joke that much of the most beautiful land remaining in this country today was considered worthless a century ago when our Indian tribes were banished to it. Now that land is about the last beautiful quasi-unspoiled terrain we've got on which to sustain our spirits. And in the middle of the night I'll suddenly bolt upright into a sitting position thinking: Wow! What kind of a fantastic country might this be today if such lousy capitalists as them had been the caretakers of the land these past two hundred years!

So I wish I could move slowly, savoring my existence in this rural place. But I can't. For many reasons this picturesque valley does not have the power to do that. And though for miles every moment of every inch of this land is experienced by the eye like bursting out of a tunnel upon an ocean, I still walk around confounded and confused, aching because of this emotional or political failure or that business disaster, worried about deadlines, worried about children, worried about the car breaking down. Then, when I look up — behold! Suddenly the view is so wide I must syncopate a step, hesitate in conversation, apply the brakes: for I'm honestly startled. I mean, how can I feel like I feel — low, mean, and ugly — when all this is around me?

But it cannot really slow me down or stop me. Or, apparently, significantly change my ways or the political reality of past and current world history. Nevertheless, it gives balance.

And that has made all the difference.

We began in August of 1969 by doing little things, getting the feel of community, neighbors, rhythm.

The house had five rooms: white insulation board formed a false ceiling. Across the driveway, an adobe shack once used as a smokehouse and chicken coop had been gutted when some brooders caught fire.

Naturally, the first thing people do to make a place their own is renovate. It's good therapy too, for quashing those New York City blues. So right off the bat we tackled the ceilings and walls and the chicken coop.

View from the Frances Martin house, Lower Ranchitos

Aspen sprig and roots near
Picuris Peak

A hollow mortarboard wall divided the area now known as the living room. We knocked on the wall, decided it wasn't holding up anything crucial, and proceeded to demolish it with an ax and a sledgehammer. Later, it occurred to me we probably could have dismantled the wall the same way it had gone up, coming out of the exercise with some valuable wallboard and good two-by-four framing. But back then we were hot to go and tense from a lot of pent-up megalopolitan hostility, so we laid right in and had a ball.

Next, the ugly false ceiling — at least in the living room and our bedroom — had to go. We tore it down in five minutes, exposing lovely old beams. The insulation board went to panel an outhouse beside the garage shack; the rest we carted to the dump. (An old egg-laying box wound up in the outhouse: we cut a small hole in the bottom of the outhouse door, threw up some chicken wire for a pen, and paid a buck apiece for arthritic three-year-old hens, who laid a few eggs, brightened up the yard as they puttered around, and were soon butchered by neighborhood dogs.)

After destroying the living room wall and ripping down the false ceiling, we varnished floor and ceiling beams, then paused to admire our handiwork.

We could hear a very disquieting sound, a tiny, sibilant sprinkle as of fine earthen particles — perhaps sand — splashing like gossamer mist upon the floor. Glancing up, eyes suspiciously squinted, we inspected cracks between ceiling cross-boards, and immediately discovered the raison d'être of that fiberboard we had so cavalierly destroyed. Eight inches of roofing dirt was sprinkling through cracks onto our heads! A neighbor I consulted about this phenomenon said in the old days poor people often laid down only a single layer of newspaper on the roof before adding the dirt. Over the years, naturally, the newspaper rotted away, and for that reason in many Taos houses dirt sifts steadily into the rooms like sand from an hourglass. "If you got the money," my neighbor said, "what I would do is buy a bunch of those white fiberboard squares and construct a false ceiling. Otherwise, the dust raining onto your head every day and night will drive you crazy."

Shortly thereafter, I turned the scorched chicken coop into an office. Concluding that a foot of dirt roof offered scant protection for my paperback books and manuscripts, I took a few swift measurements, jotted down some calculations, or-dered a mess of finish-grade T-and-G lumber, and, moments following delivery, went right to work.

Admittedly, you can't get much more expensive than finish-grade tongue-and-groove lumber. Worth its weight in gold, the stuff is the kind of material that might have paneled Louis XIV's master bedroom. But to use it for protection over a foot-thick dirt roof that couldn't leak anyway is absurd.

No matter — my ignorance was blissful way back then.

A month later I knew I had goofed, however. Talk about weathertight. The roof was capped by two layers of fifteen-pound tar paper, one layer of sixty-pound paper, and a final layer of lap-sealed green granular ninety-pound roofing mate-rial. Friends in the know who dropped by to view my roof staggered backward, letting out explosive exclamations as they sputtered: "How much did that thing cost to put up anyway?" When I quoted a figure, they groaned. "Christ, man, you could have built a six-room house with plumbing for what it cost you to put a roof over this tiny little shack that didn't need extra protection in the first place!"

The old saw: I'd used a howitzer to assassinate a mosquito!

Still, my first carpentry effort was — and remains, by God! — a beautiful work of art. Building it was fun, very therapeutic, and left me glowing with accomplishment . . . until I discovered five months later that snowmelt draining from the overhang into the outhouse was liable to drown all my chickens!

And eight months later, having learned my way around the local subsistence hustles, I built a forty-foot-long, twelve-foot-wide, three-room chicken coop, complete with scav-enged picture windows, for a fifth of what it cost to raise that tiny twelve-by-fourteen peaked roof over my office.

I don't care, though. That tongue-and-groove roof is like hanging an original Picasso in an outhouse, and, in my better moments, I dig the arrogance involved.

I also know beyond a doubt that the massive heaps of confetti (formerly my precious books and manuscripts) created by the piranha mice of Ranchitos will never be dam-pened by a single drop of pernicious rainwater!

I loved working on that roof, straining to wedge those tongues into their proper grooves, pausing often to watch summer happening around me, sweating off pounds every day, working with the smell of meadow grass and clean pine lumber in my nostrils. I loved the feel of that wood, and the symmetry involved in the job. Most of all, I enjoyed my evening fatigue. It was no exhaustion created by tension: I was pooped from simple constructive physical labor, a sensation similar to one I always had after athletic practice in college, a pleasant tiredness I've come to know well again in Taos, where living with land and errant houses needing care means plenty of hard labor. Yet when a natural strife produces that fatigue, for me, at my tender age, it's a real gift I want to guard carefully, never losing it again. For those who even partially survive off the land in an area like Taos, where farming can be the original sadomasochistic trip, I grant that it's a hard life. But I would imagine that usually the toil is somehow meaningful, if only for that special fatigue at dusk; if only because the work is what has unified the community for centuries, making life stable and worthwhile.

I paused often, raising that roof. For once in my life I had plenty of time. After Ruby handed up an icy beer, I'd relax, watching Ranchitos activities taking place on or near surrounding pastureland, small adobe houses, cottonwood trees, and barbed-wire fence lines.

One evening a flight of winged ants started dropping onto me and onto the pine planks. They fell in twos, stuck together at the abdomen, copulating. For minutes they floated around me like snow. A sudden and strange little happening, it made me feel loose and happy inside. Dusty mist from the nearby dirt road hovered lightly above the fields like a transparent scarf. Thunderheads grumbled above Taos Mountain, spitting jagged lightning. In a moment it rained for fifteen minutes. Big drops splattering against the driveway made the air redolent with an evocative smell of damp dust. Following the shower, a double rainbow was born. Clearly exposed in its entirety, the arc arose from mountains north of Taos near the small village of Arroyo Seco, curved high over Taos Mountain, the Pueblo, and Taos proper, and touched again south of Llano Quemado, about thirty miles from where it began.

Or do rainbows travel from south to north?

Luke, Ruby, and I entered the back field in order to see it better. Slowly, the thing dissolved: evening pacified the valley. The sky was so many shades of blue and gray and burnt pink and umber it seemed patently ridiculous. A little selectivity, please, Nuevo Mejico! Liza Minnelli once told me she tries never to cry in a song: on the grounds that some emotion must be left for listeners' imaginations. Our southwestern sky has no such discipline: it's all or nothing every day until we are so gorged on beauty we damn near vomit!

Nighthawks came out, nearly invisible except for a single white stripe across each wing, making it possible to trace their jerky erratic flight. Later, we walked a hundred yards along the dirt road to Sebastian's Bar for a six-pack of beer. An enormous bar, full of empty space like the land, it had a pay pool game, a few tables and chairs. A couple of guys were always playing eight ball. Perhaps another person sat on a stool. A song might be playing on the jukebox — most of the music came from Albuquerque and featured Al Hurricane, Baby Gaby, Tiny Morrie. Behind the bar sat old Sebastian himself, originally from Spain and now dying, eyes growing milky and dim. He liked to reach out, touching Luke's lemon-yellow Afro for luck.

On returning, six-pack in hand, from Sebastian's after our first rainbow, we glanced up at the stars, of course, and were properly awed by the natural clarity surrounding our New Lives. Dew had dampened roadbed dust, the sky was incredibly clear. The Big Dipper's bowl just touched the silvery tips of poplars along the river. Oystershell scale disease is killing the Ranchitos cottonwoods, but we didn't know that then. Our neighbor's horses snorted as we ambled by; we snorted back at them. We could hear the river, and irrigation water bubbled through short-cropped grass.

Seated on our portal, we drank the beer. Moths fluttered against the kitchen windows. Standing on a chair, Luke grabbed for them. The underwings were among the largest; hidden beneath their ordinary gray wing was a large vermilion splotch. Nearby, tiny diaphanous green moths clung to the screen door.

Thunder rumbled like the proverbial faraway big guns way down south around the Jemez.

And I believed that when I got up, six years of New York tension would have drained from my body, making a spot on the concrete portal where I'd been.

But that never happened.

No problem, though. The belief that it could or might happen was all that mattered. For given the nature of this valley, nobody could stay shell-shocked forever.

Tree bark, Llano Quemado orchard

High country west of Taos

Almost immediately after unlocking the front door and taking possession, we traveled south to renew acquaintances with Justin Locke, the man whose house I had visited for a week during my first summer out West: instantly, we became fast friends.

Summertime being Justin's season, he was always enthusiastically hoeing, irrigating, fixing his roof, killing ants, pruning, harvesting, caulking, clipping — you name it. And sneezing nonstop, his eyes watering from the wide variety of lovely grasses clinging to his terraced hillsides. He also spent hours on his front portal constructing strange galactic canvases from a gruesome variety of polyurethane poisons, merrily breathing in dozens of cancer-causing, liver-destroying, heart-palpitating, brain-damaging vapors while at his work overlooking that serene valley.

Just sitting on his evening hillside was an adventure. Sheep bells clanked lazily. Magpies and other birds drifted among the cool orchard trees below. White beehives gave character to several fields. Occasionally, a pickup truck chugged along a dirt road crossing the valley, trailing a wake of dust that spread out woozily on either side of the road, in slow motion. Sunflowers bloomed: several untended fields looked solidly yellow. In other fields, green alfalfa plants were almost obliterated by a blanket of their own purple flowers.

Somebody had peacocks. Their cries occasionally echoed down the narrow valley like the cry of a cat in pain or in heat. Though considered an unlucky bird in a superstitious country, there are nevertheless some folks who keep them around. These people suffer premature heart attacks and strokes, their children are paralyzed in auto accidents, their horses succumb to equine encephalitis, their chickens lay eggs whose shells break when they are picked up — but still they persist in harboring peacocks. The Job complex is alive and well and living in Taos, New Mexico!

Walking onto the mesa behind Justin's house, we sat down on rocks among sagebrush plants and juniper trees, buffeted gently by warm evening winds, gazing westward at the usual disgustingly apropos sunset. Overhead a few bats, swallows, and nighthawks did their thing. Traveling southwest toward the Jemez, our eyes always focused on miniature Pedernal, the mesa mountain of Abiquiu, as special in its way as our own hill, important — given its special shape among rounded mountains — distinctly attractive.

I helped Justin irrigate his place. It was like splashing water over a twenty-tiered wedding cake. Channels and little acequias led every which way, looping into this lawn, a garden, fruit trees, gurgling through an intricate system of ditches that zigzagged everywhere, dropping from one terraced level to the next like an aquatic Slinky — a fabulous, also demented, arterial system, managed by a madman.

Justin stabbed his shovel into the earth, and presto! the apricot tree by the bedroom had enough to drink for another two weeks. He opened a tiny wooden head gate, and a crimson vine — like a beautiful, insidious thing from Rappaccini's garden — breathed deeply. If he plunked a rock in the Y where a small ditch diverged, water bypassed his cellar door, circled a beehive oven and a tool shed, shot part of its wad in a garden choked with bionic greenery, and plunged downhill to make soggy a cliff of timothy so thick even a snake couldn't slither through it.

Another diversion tumbled water over a rock ledge into thick grass on the narrow open area just before the valley drop-off in front of the house. Stripping naked, we cavorted in the icy waterfall, gasping. Then stood glistening on the edge of the sharp hill, hands on our hips, overlooking the fertile world — overplayed, arrogant, opulent, a scene straight out of a Ken Russell movie or an Ayn Rand novel, Justin all brown beside me, and myself white as a snowflake against the verdant mood, aspen leaves clattering soundlessly in the background like a trillion deaf-mute bells.

Sound idyllic? In ways it was — in bits and pieces. But Taos was not gained in a day. Too often, I worried on paper about the processes of sensibility: after New York, a death seemed trapped in my heart. I couldn't really grab the moments, allowing them to impart fulfillment.

Herewith, some of my tuppenny diary philosophizing from those days:

If you don't make an effort to consciously place yourself within a moment and appreciate it, then you just don't have it [I wrote on August 21, 1969.] To enjoy takes more than just letting things happen to you. Christ, I must be getting so spiritually lazy! When you are aware, everything can be enjoyable. But I seem to have closed so much of that off. I keep myself preoccupied with worry about things, and don't dig what's around me. I don't think enough about what's going on. I really haven't talked to anybody about *ideas* in ages. Not that I'm unhappy here. I'm just not really tuned into life in a positive way. Isolated incidents occur that are beautiful, but I can't weave them into everyday patterns that give the feeling of a continuity of positive living. I'm lazy about living. Hey, shouldn't *everything* be a miracle?

I envied my friend Justin, the intense way he tackled life. Noisy, brash, loudmouthed — he had a flair for the dramatic, the obnoxious, the passionate, the stupid. The aroma from a chunk of dry horse dung could so excite him he would almost pull an ecstatic fainting spell. He could hoe beans with the orgiastic flair most people reserve for their special adulteries. He talked, blustered, exclaimed, and groaned, one minute suicidal, the next moment ready to flip out from sheer delight. A painter, a maniacal (messianical) horticulturist, a hotshot photographer, a peripatetic womanizer, an Amway salesman, a speaker of volatile French, Spanish, and English, a substitute teacher, a fossil hunter — I thought Justin had it all. I loved just to sit watching his facial expressions, listening to his vocabulary cluttered with "old boy" and "gruesome" and "you sweet thing." He would roar into the mountains, sketching windblown pines, then hurry back and train tiny Bonzai trees to grow in the image of his sketches. He drank a can of beer at a single gulp, and on an impulse would frantically fill up plastic bags with apricots for us to carry home. Wrapped in a blanket, he often walked barefoot on the mesa, letting wind whip his hair and flap the blanket around him as if he were trapped inside the aerodynamics of wings. Raw fish and tartare meat smothered in garlic consituted his diet. A health faddist, Justin also smoked cigarettes and sometimes drank a bottle of good bourbon a night while writing wild poetry. And although approaching his fifties, he had the lean, muscled body of a twenty-year-old.

As for myself, unable to sustain an enjoyment of my new environment, I often felt trapped in the flesh of a fifty-year-old. Many times I soaked in the bathtub after dark, worrying because my life lacked energy; and my writing seemed lackluster, unemotional, dull. I found it an enormously tiring ritual, often so boring I wanted to scream. I did entire novels feeling so desperate that sometimes I was actually crying as words went down on paper. It felt as if I was working on the memory of creativity, rather than the real thing.

So I sat in the bathtub feeling numb, wishing that I could learn again to love my work; and my everyday existence. Pears were ripening on the old tree outside a small window over my head. Moths battered all over the place — small, dull-colored, frantic. Bouncing off the ceiling, they landed on their backs in my steaming bathwater, wriggling helplessly as I watched them die. Slowly they drifted around on currents caused by my slow breathing, trailing thin lines of powder that expanded slowly, dissolving. Autumn came through the window: I could smell it everywhere. I had to work hard to keep a maudlin furrowed brow, because fall always excites me. That early pre-chill, that faint hint of frost, is like a sign of life: wake up, world, it's time for action again!

¡Que viva la muerte!

One evening Ruby came in and sat down — back from a trip to Española. Enthusiastically, she described her journey to the Puye Cliff Ruins. The road was flanked by scarlet spiky flowers beleaguered by hummingbirds. She had not seen, in all her lifetime, as many hummingbirds as lined the road that day, buzzing like tiny chain saws. Then she described the drive back, through Velarde, the Rio Grande Gorge, and the wide fabulous mesa leading home.

Velarde is a fruit town located thirty miles south of here at the mouth of the gorge, some fifteen miles north of Española. Wet and green, most of its old adobe houses are hidden among acres of fruit trees. Along the highway, stands sell apples, pears, peaches, red chile ristras — you name it. Impossible not to stop and load up on fruit before zooming between those high canyon walls onto one of the more dangerous stretches of highway I know, two lanes of twisting macadam with cliffs (and rock slides) on one side, and the Rio Grande on the other at the bottom of a thirty-foot, hundred-foot, three-hundred-foot topple down boulder-strewn slopes.

Aspen grove at Justin Locke's house

Aspen by an irrigation ditch,
Llano Quemado

Occasionally, the narrow canyon widens to accommodate picturesque little villages that must spend half their days in shadow: Embudo, Rinconada, Pilar. In Embudo, there was a small hospital where our daughter Tania would be born in about a year. In Rinconada, a famous worm farm always intrigued the kids: it has since relocated to Velarde, where two worm farms on opposite sides of the road fanatically grow their crops in order to supply Bill Vickers at Sierra Sporting Goods of Taos with enough natural bait to seriously deplete the Rio Grande of its large trout, bass, carp, sucker, and pickerel population.

Across the Rio Grande, as you head north from Velarde, there's an old path chopped against the western gorge walls, the former railbed of a narrow-gauge train that climbed beside the river, then veered west atop the mesa heading for a station at tiny La Servilleta, some thirty miles closer to the setting sun than Taos. My friend Andrés Martínez remembers taking that train sixty years ago. Sometimes they hitched horses to the engine, helping it up the steeper grades: passengers debarked and walked behind the train to lighten the load.

Ruby was full of enthusiasm about the journey: Luke had liked best the enormous tent caterpillar colonies killing gigantic cottonwood trees beside the Rio Grande. Then, after telling me about their day, Ruby thrust out her hand: she was pinching a seed-like mass of pearly-palomino-colored fiber not much bigger than a quarter. And when she relaxed the pressure of her fingers, the fibers expanded miraculously, the fluff bulged, spreading open, and suddenly a thousand minute feathery tufts took weightless flight, filling the bathroom air with a beautiful wispy fairy down.

Just a magic plant she had discovered by the side of the road, among all the hummingbirds!

Abruptly — saved by the bell! — I felt myself expanding like that ridiculous seed ball, growing instantly light-headed and happy, all at once buoyed by the fact that I had escaped New York City intact, landing in an environment where I could be startled constantly by a natural phenomenon like this having roots in a special landscape not yet destroyed by progressive human endeavors.

Such moments often took me by surprise back then. They also accumulated, eating away at my neuroses, making me vulnerable to enchantment again.

Shortly after landing in our Taos house, we bought a refrigerator, made sure the water heater functioned, promptly coopified the outhouse because we already had an indoor toilet, and installed a butane heater in the living room. When it came to purchasing a kitchen stove, however, we bought a fifth-hand combination gas and wood-burning outfit — a real country appliance, and the cheapest stove we could find. Scrounging a little more, we located two small old-fashioned cast-iron wood heaters, installing one in our bedroom, the other in my office. And, as a kind of auxiliary heating system to the living room's butane heater, we paid twelve bucks for one of those tin stoves that require a few inches of sand on the oval bottom and last maybe five years.

Unknown to us then, setting up that kind of heating system was giving us a good excuse to spend the rest of our lives gathering, chopping, and burning wood.

Occasionally, it seems as if these are really the only three major activities that occur in the Taos Valley. Roughly speaking, half the inhabitants seem to spend eight hours a day traveling to designated wood-gathering areas in decrepit vehicles, and then trying to guide their overloaded pickups back home without getting stuck, blowing tires on '52 Chevys with no spares, or dive-bombing off narrow roads into the gorge.

Once home, the next eight hours of half the population's days are concerned with mangling the wood into fireplace-sized chunks for burning. This is usually done with an ax and a wedge, or a chain saw. Some old-timers prefer hooking up circular-saw blades to the flywheels of their tractors. A wealthy few in the valley have either constructed or purchased hydraulic log splitters. These people are usually professional firewood gatherers; they sell to everybody else in town who doesn't have the means or the time to go wood hunting on their own.

Taos is such a wood-burning town, in fact, that for a while it was international headquarters for the Stickler, the poor man's log splitter, a large metal screw which, when bolted onto the rear wheel of a jacked-up pickup truck, can split all the wood you want in half the time for a quarter of the price.

But for most folks, such luxurious technology is a pipe dream, and they spend a lot of time out at the woodpile building up their deltoids and cursing piñon trees.

Eight years ago, I'll admit, that exercise seemed like a semi-attractive proposition to me. I had left New York starved for honest manual labor. Heaving an ax could keep my body (and its soul) in good condition, and provide free heating to boot. Today, after eight years of swinging an ax, and especially after the past bitter winter, I'd just as soon fling my ax into the well, sprinkle paint remover on the remains of my woodpile and light it, and buy a butane heater for every nook and cranny of my disintegrating adobe — to hell with the cost!

One thing that stops me from doing this is the price of butane, which keeps my hands decently enough callused so that maybe I won't be among the first put up against the wall after the revolution has triumphed.

Too, there's a mystique around here about gathering wood. By now I'm so brainwashed that I think if for some reason I could not gather and chop and burn I would immediately suffer a severe identity crisis. Admittedly, I'm no longer the purist I once was, traveling miles to find perfect piñon, burning only the best. Nowadays, I'll put anything to the torch, just as long as it is easy to find and simple to bust apart. My woodpile is the slum woodpile of Taos. I don't even sharpen my ax any more because most of the stuff I gather is so dead and dry it'll bust apart if you just give it a smart little tap. Where before I used to select only the best piñon, now I simply gather slash beside the streams I'm fishing. Which means I'm being warmed by five-year-old alamo, rotten Chinese elm, fluffy aspen, and weathered ponderosa the weight and consistency of Styrofoam. My friends shake their heads slowly, going "Tch-tch, poor John."

For them, my descent has been like watching a confirmed but classy alcoholic slip from a bottle a day of Wild Turkey 101 to six pints daily of Golden Glo rotgut sherry!

Never judge the past by what the future became, however. In the beginning, we gathered wood a few times and liked it, clinging to the ritual because it helped mute New York and focus New Mexico, and for a while we really did it correctly.

Back then they had a Big Jack operating on the other side of Carson, west of the Rio Grande Gorge, south of Tres Orejas Mountain and the infamous Carson Reservoir — built in the thirties by the U.S. government — which never held water. "They" was, still is, for that matter, the Forest Service. A three-story-high, metal-rollered tree-crunching machine, the Big Jack was leveling a piñon forest so the area could be reseeded for grazing. The leveling was an attempt to defuse local resentment over government grazing policies by creating new grasslands so local ranchers might increase their herds for a change, instead of always having to reduce them.

In short, the Big Jack was on a propaganda mission.

As far as I know today, the grass seeded over there never took very well. And half the new permits created went to big-time Colorado operators. Hence, the project has not exactly assuaged local resentments. Nevertheless, to clear all that valuable slash (instead of burning it or carting it out at government expense), people were allowed to go in and lug it away gratis.

Talk about piñon manna from heaven! To expedite matters, not only did the Big Jack topple the forest, but its bladed rollers also chopped whole trees into fireplace-sized chunks, eliminating countless hours of ax work. All we had to do was collect it, take it home, and throw it into the fire.

We went often, and the hard work felt mighty good. The spectacular drive over was occasionally offset by a dangerous return journey, but the rhythm and mood of the activity made up for everything. That wood gathering facilitated our New York withdrawal, it calmed us a bit, allowing experimentation with other gears to see which new one might help us accelerate into the next stage of existence.

To get to where the Big Jack was leveling and conveniently packaging the forest, we followed Ranchitos Road around the western edge of the valley to Los Córdovas, turned right onto the mesa, dropped into the Rio Grande Gorge, and pushed twenty miles beyond. Ranchitos Road itself is one of the more beautiful routes I have ever traveled. For half its length the road pretty much follows the course of the Pueblo River, and so far the land on either side is not overly developed. Pastureland is low, lush, dotted with animals; cottonwood trees are few and far between, hence visibility is wide, and wildlife abounds.

Los Córdovas I know little about. The southwesternmost and least developed satellite town of Taos, it makes a lovely picture of how small Spanish towns used to be as you jounce by on the horrible dirt road bisecting its cluster of adobe houses. In many small pastures horses, cattle, and sheep are always grazing. There are no billboards, and no commercial

Grazing in the Ranchos Valley

The view from El Prado, just north of Taos

enterprises. The acequias are well cared for, and most of the land is still under cultivation—rural, rustic, productive.

My friends Bob Bishop and Bonnie Korman live in Los Córdovas. They bought an old ruin, and, despite the propensity of young married couples to file for divorce during the traumatic experience of building in Taos, they survived the renovation; a miracle, given the odds against it. Perhaps, then, a kind of protective shield guards Los Córdovas because it is a less complicated, more serene and old-fashioned village.

Nobody takes this kind of survival for granted, though. In past years Los Córdovans fought hard to defeat town efforts to build a new sewage plant directly in their midst. And I have a feeling they will fight again to stop developers from building a golf course in their community, irrigating its greens and fairways with sewage water from the new plant currently located about a half mile south of the outermost Los Córdovas family.

The rationale for their protest is simple. Few in Los Córdovas can afford golfing equipment, let alone the time for playing the game. The project is totally an outsiders' deal, a plaything of the middle class. Sooner or later, should the golf course succeed, the players will clamor for a paved road so their new cars won't suffer on the way to the game. But paving speeds up vehicles, pollutes air, threatens children. It also increases taxes. Likewise, a paved road raises land values, which in turn increases taxes. The golf course itself inflates neighboring land prices, gratuitously upping taxes yet again, putting increased pressure on local people to sell their land for enormous sums to loaded outsiders wishing to live in the wonderful southwestern sun next door to a golf course. The weakest, oldest, or most impoverished members of the community succumb first. The terrain they sell is usually retired from agricultural production, becoming split-level ranch homes, maybe developments. The developments further increase land values and property taxes, seriously straining the financial resources of the people, many of whom knock down less than three grand cash a year. Fields no longer planted for forage, or seeded for gardens, place a steadily growing strain on the surrounding dwindling agricultural infrastructure. Each property sold to a non-farmer means less grass neighbors can rent for their cattle or buy for baling. It means one less irrigator and conscientious dues-payer on the ditch system: one less person taking a crucial active political part in the community. As the town fills with non-Spanish speakers and inhabitants unsympathetic to the local culture, society, and economics, bonds that have solidified the Spanish-speaking community weaken. Together, their financial system carefully balanced within a bartering economy, the poor ranchers of Los Córdovas have survived for centuries. But once forced into a *sauve qui peut*, private enterprise, capitalist, progress-American-style hysteria, their marginal subsistence will become submarginal: within a decade they'll be gone.

All this on a simple scenic drive along a bucolic road in search of wood?

And more. As we shall later see.

Beyond Los Córdovas the dirt road rises onto the mesa, continuing for a while along a sagebrush plain where, if you look closely, you can see the grid patterns of subdivisions plotted many years ago, but never realized. A right turn, and five more miles of dirt road heading due west carry you to the rim of the Pueblo Gorge.

Perhaps it was a sunny day, clear and cloudless: more often uncertain weather threatened rain, thunder rumbling—the rainy season always added a sense of peril to our wood runs. Dry, the mesa roads were fine. Only slightly wet, they became slicker than ice. Even at two miles an hour we could slide out of control into a ditch, stuck in the middle of a momentarily heartless desolation.

There being few trees on the mesa, the panorama was total. At the rim of the Pueblo Gorge we often stopped, looking back at the entire high plain, the green valleys, the mountains. Taos Mountain might be supremely lit in strange white sunlight. But at the same time it would be raining in the Talpa hills, pouring so hard a mist of silvery explosions outlined the ridges of those gentle hills.

Turning left, we descended precipitously: for the next few miles any slight miscalculation meant a five-hundred-foot tumble down a steep slope into the narrow Pueblo River cascading rapidly among smoothly sculptured granite boulders toward the Rio Grande.

A narrow bridge crossed the Rio Grande. Gourd-shaped mud nests of cliff swallows clung against the concrete pillars under the roadbed. Rising on the other side, the road performed scary switchbacks, threading between enormous reddish-brown boulders. Often buzzards plied the special currents twisting between the canyon walls.

For a mile, across the western mesa, stretched a wide colony of large anthills. Then sagebrush took over again, and that summer its color was spectacularly evocative — almost iridescent, pastel blue-green-ash-purple, impossible to pinpoint except that it made me ache it was so lovely. Clumps of snakeweed bloomed yellow in the sage: sometimes entire fields of the low round bushes were beautifully interspersed with fuzzy blond foxtail. For a while the road continued level, sage bordering either side. Tiny cinnamon-colored ground squirrels darted across our path. A small adobe ruin slid by. Farther on we passed a corral of shiny gray fence posts, big tumbleweeds stuck between the posts. Suddenly, two old houses made of stone appeared; wrecked automobiles sank into a sandy yard; piles of piñon wood were high as the houses.

A dip in the mesa: we twisted and dropped a hundred feet into a wash where sage grew taller, less dusty; and high rabbit brush beside the road was a vibrant spring-apple green. A handful of cows dumbly observed our honking approach: it took them forever to saunter stupidly off to the side.

Suddenly it began hailing; white stones about a third the size of my pinkie fingernail bounced on the dirt road, falling slanted so that they seemed to race ahead of the car. His hand stuck out the window, Luke grabbed the hail, laughing. Seconds later, we reached sunshine again. Then wind raised channels of dust ahead that swirled along inches off the ground in front of us like snakes rapidly fleeing our advance.

Nearing Route 285, we turned left onto a raised bed that used to be the narrow-gauge trestle heading for La Servilleta. For the next few miles we zoomed along at a fast clip, straddling deep ruts, praying not to catch a tire and have a blowout or break an axle or flip over. This five-mile suicide run carried us to the desolate country of the Big Jack, where an entire forest was leveled and a dusty silence might be broken only by the shadow of dreamy vultures circling a mile above it all.

Yet that desolation had a tremendous richness given special intensity by our labor. The isolation, the aspects of holocaust, were beautiful. Given the fragile, wide land, all life and weather seemed notoriously special. One day, clumps of brittle roadside grasses swarmed with silky gray caterpillars.

Next day, the lifeless area was spooky, church-like, unreal. Unhurriedly, we gathered wood in hot silence, surrounded by surreal weather. In the east over by Taos rain lifted off the mountains, a herd of fluffy clouds retreating up and away from pitch-black hills. Between the mountains and the rain clouds, a lovely yellow sky melted into aqua tones, limpid and clear. Directly over our heads, a dozen shades of gray merging in a subtle gouache kept shifting with underplayed dramatic effects. A funny thunder, muttering and sighing inarticulately, puttered around in the sky. As the day died, a few big raindrops fell, but no deluge occurred. As night deepened to the east, the air became curiously vibrant: Luke's lemony-white hair glowed as if on fire. To the west gray clouds framed sunny patches of horizon sky: nearby, falling rain was a rouge mist stretching for miles. Every minute jagged lightning flickered down through the gentle smirrh and faint thunder boomed.

Standing in darkness, we watched this show. Bunches of purple flowers dotting the desolation were lit up by the electric darkness like underwater neon bouquets. Barely able to see each other, we gathered final armloads of piñon. Only a streak of horizon was visible, like the light shining from under a heavy theater curtain after the houselights have gone out, just before the curtain rises. A radiant streak a hundred miles long, its clean emerald-green sky was broken at intervals by heavy black clouds out of which delicate gauzy strokes of pink rain were falling.

In darkness we left, sucking on fat peaches. Halfway to Carson, the road became slippery from rain. I slowed until the car was in first gear. Back and forth we slithered, proceeding for long stretches turned nearly sideways. Ditches on either side carried water; big puddles filled each dip in the dirt road; kangaroo rats, excited by the storm, scurried back and forth. At the gorge, the descending road had been nearly washed out in places. At one point it seemed to be wrenching off the cliffside: sickening cracks barred the way. Trying to straddle a deep rut, the car slid sideways, and it appeared we would be hung up for good. Getting out, I pushed, Ruby swung us clear of the ditch, straddled another crevasse, and somehow we sloshed safely by.

East of the gorge, the mesa road was dry. Lazy grasshoppers and moths floated through our headlight beams. The fear we had experienced ten minutes ago had never happened.

Early winter, Ranchos de Taos

A magic plant from Taos Canyon

The weather here is abrupt like that, occasionally dangerous. On a bone-dry day a mesa arroyo can suddenly hold a flash flood from a rain ten miles away in the foothills. Sunny days and cloudless skies often erupt into violent rainstorms, making roads that have been passable for months impassable within minutes. Once, on a dry day after a wood run, our car sank up to the axles in damp sand that had looked to be perfectly dry — it took hours to dig ourselves out. In mid-July in the high country I have awakened to discover thin films of ice on lakes that the previous day I fished in seventy-degree heat. Hiking into Bear Lake on a becalmed summer day at the start of September three years ago, I was caught in a blizzard.

We never knew what "New England weather" really was like until we moved to Taos County!

Returning from our wood runs, we often stopped for a swim in the Pueblo River. Parking on the dirt road fifty feet above the river, we climbed down the embankment, stripped naked, and slipped into the water. The widest pools measured only fifteen or twenty feet across: none was more than four feet deep. Shaped like chairs and tubs, boulders were black and seal-smooth. Seated under small waterfalls, we let icy water splash over our heads. And floated in the lime-white froth of a succession of natural whirlpool baths: it was like bathing in beer or sparkling ginger ale. Battered old pickups, so loaded with logs their tailgates were dragging, chugged dustily up the road above us: laconic suntanned arms waved.

We should have realized that we could easily offend long-time local residents with our skinny-dipping hippie ways. However, feeling far away from the road, and always careful to keep largely submerged, we did not think ourselves a bother. A year later, however, the lesson was driven home forever. I went down in the Pueblo Gorge with my sister-in-law, my children, and her two kids — all of them under six. By then I knew the score, and everybody wore a bathing suit. For a while, we had an idyllic time. Seated on a rock, I leafed through a magazine, one eye cocked on the kids wading in a shallow run gathering pebbles, splashing each other. Upstream, my sister-in-law cast for trout with my fly rod. Forty feet overhead an old red car stopped, two drunk men got out, gathered some large rocks, and began heaving them at us. At first, thinking it a joke, we waved. Angrily, the men yelled obscenities and aimed to hit us. Suddenly we realized they wanted to commit murder. Unable to escape or seek shelter, we shouted at the kids, herding them frantically together, and pushed them ahead of us downstream, trying to flee. Understanding the nature of the danger immediately, the children plunged ahead, splashing through the water, scrambling over rocks, never hesitating for a second. Above, the men followed along for a ways, screaming and methodically pelting down the rocks, any one of which, had it struck a head, would have meant sure death. Several times we yanked a child out of the way, or shoved somebody into the water to avoid a missile. After tracking us for fifty yards, the men abruptly quit, storming back to their car, and drove away. Nobody had been hurt. The entire incident had taken two minutes. Brightly and peacefully the sun was shining: brown trout quietly undulated against the pebbly bottom of the clean pool where we had halted.

Human relationships here, then, can be like the weather. In a landscape where so much organic peace seems constantly to loom benevolently over us all, there exists the same North America as in Cleveland or Boston, or New York's Lower East Side. Blue mountains, mauve sagebrush terrain, and pink rain falling have nothing whatever to do with the system guiding our society through it all.

On a wood run in late September we finally ran into our first rattlesnake. When we moved out West, I had assumed these snakes would be all over the place. But so far, after eight years' tramping about the countryside, fishing every conceivable terrain in this county, I have seen exactly four rattlers. They may be around, all right, but they are scared stiff of human beings, and with good reason.

This particular snake lay on the dirt road near Carson, west of the gorge. Darkness falling, we were puttering along slowly, enjoying the usual voluptuous view replete with crimson and flamingo-pink clouds; a crescent moon occupied a serene amethyst heaven. Noticing the snake, I braked, killed the engine but left our lights on, and stepped out to give Luke a lesson in rattlesnake habits and identification.

Stick in hand, I approached timidly. The snake seemed groggy, reluctant to perform. I stamped my foot a few times, making it coil. "Now it'll give a warning buzz with the rattles on its tail," I informed my audience, who peered expectantly through the windshield. But the snake refused to give a warning. I waved my stick in front of it. "You'll see it strike the stick," I called over to Luke. But he saw no such thing. Coiled, soundless, the serpent maintained only a lethargic alertness. Gingerly, I tapped its snout: only then did it strike the stick — I jumped back a mile, taken by surprise.

Then it vented some anger, giving off a high tenor buzz.

Back in the car, I circled the snake and pressed on. Moments later, a pickup sped past us, a man and his son waving cheerfully: they were gone in a cloud of dust. Slowing down, I said, "I'll bet they killed that snake." Out of curiosity we U-turned and went back to see.

They had. It was beside the road, smashed and chopped into several pieces.

Sometimes, returning from our first wood runs, we forsook the Taos Junction road and traveled north on 285 to Tres Piedras, then drove southeast on Route 111 in order to pass over the bridge spanning the top of the gorge. No fences ran along the road, and cattle roamed freely. The mesa up there is antelope country, and one day I saw a herd of twenty-five racing across the quiet plain, the first of those animals I had ever seen in the wilderness. Stopping the car, I felt locked in an African vista. Every few miles a lone juniper cast a dramatic black silhouette. Above the antelope the full moon was as transparently white as a thin wafer of ice.

Later I stopped at the gorge bridge. The gorge was dark; seven hundred feet below, the Rio Grande trickle was a shiny, lead-silver color, like a delicate vein in a black stone. I got dizzy looking down. And afraid. The fall was so great. And for some reason that silver ribbon trickling through blackness viewed from warm seven o'clock sunshine made me shudder.

Later on in the fall of that year, after every wood run we stopped in the forest beside the old railroad trestle and gathered piñon nuts. It was a good year. In forests all around Taos people collected the nuts falling from piñon cones. We spread a blanket under a tree and one of us climbed up and shook the branches. Usually, most of the nuts wound up beside, instead of on, the blanket, and we crawled on our hands and knees, plucking up the tiny brown nuts one by one, placing them in coffee cans or paper bags. At home we heated the nuts in the oven or in a frying pan: and then nibbled on them constantly for the next two years.

Suddenly, it was October. Snow had started falling in the mountains. We drove home from wood expeditions biting open the tiny piñon nut shells and sucking in the raw meat, spitting the shells out the window, our eyes fixed on the white misty configurations settling over Taos Mountain, winter occurring just above our valley, threatening to bury us all in white at any moment.

It was my habit then to stop and pick up birds and small mammals hit by other automobiles, and one day I found a bird I had never even heard of — a Williamson's sapsucker. Another time, out beyond Carson, we found a lovely tan-and-gray sage thrasher, a streamlined bird whose colors had come from this earth, but whose delicate shape seemed imported from a foreign planet.

As winter approached, we made our last run. And as the final conveniently sectioned piñon chunks were being unloaded onto the nine-foot-high woodpile beside our portal, we both thought our wood could last forever: or at least for the next two years. Mercifully unaware that we would be out of logs and half freezing to death by February, we stumbled inside, stoked up a fire in the combination stove, then soaked in a hot tub, sore and dusty and smelling of piñon pitch, our bodies woozy and, in that steamy water, voluptuously dreamy. Dressing in starched clean clothes, we cooked up a steak and ate baked potatoes with sour cream, had cabbage on the side, and drank beer. Moths had quit battering around the portal light bulb: all the valley trees had turned — their leaves were starting to fall.

In bed on crinkly clean white sheets, the window open, we lay quiet, listening to the valley, smelling apples and pears rotting in our little orchard; and getting faint whiffs also of the snow gathering in the mountains.

I have never loved any moment any better.

During black early-morning hours of October 12, the first snow fell. Luke came into the bedroom shortly after sunrise and woke me up. Together, we knelt on the dou-

Pueblo River gorge near confluence with Rio Grande

Rocks in arroyo below Los Córdovas

7 1

ble bed, gazing out the window, Ruby and a cat still asleep beside us. Our little lawn was almost white: a fine green gauze atop the snow was made by tips of grass. In the orchard a thousand crimson crab apples wore perfect cones of snow. Starlings in the high cottonwoods behind the office-garage made a racket. The yellow foliage of those trees was bleached by the clinging snow.

Chickadees hung upside down from bent, crisp sunflowers beyond the clothesline. A Lewis' woodpecker hammered on a nearby Chinese elm.

Luke and I got dressed, started a fire in the kitchen stove, and went outside. Clouds lay in smoky streaks across the green and white mountains. Rich blue piñon and cedar smoke rose from chimneys all over town. We admired the weather for a moment, then drove into Taos, and, in the popcorn-scented Rexall Drugstore, bought the Sunday papers—the Albuquerque *Journal*, the Santa Fe *New Mexican*, the *Rocky Mountain News*.

Back home, we languished over sausages and hot muffins, reading the newspaper. Then I took a bird from the refrigerator freezing compartment, let it thaw, and skinned and stuffed it, hanging it by a thread from the living-room ceiling. Already suspended from that ceiling were two ferocious-looking great horned owls, a nighthawk, a sharp-shinned hawk, a magpie, and a shrike. While I skinned and stuffed, Ruby baked chocolate-chip cookies, and we watched the Mets play Baltimore in the miracle World Series. Jerry Koosman pitched a two-hitter, winning the tense game 2−1. Nervous wrecks afterward, we went outside and picked a basket of pears, then went for a walk up Ranchitos Road.

Snow fell lightly again; although only midafternoon, an overcast sky made it dark and crepuscular. Just beyond the small Ranchitos church, six blackface sheep grazed on Bernardo Trujillo's front lawn, their bells clinking quietly. A few yards farther along a group of Indian ponies in a wide Pueblo pasture rested quietly as snow built up on their backsides. Killdeers—invisible in the gloom—screeched all around them.

Memories of that type of moment are powerful enough to break my heart a little. The family is no longer together. And Bernardo Trujillo, a friend who helped teach me about the acequia politics and held our ditch together against the onslaught of apathy and "progress," died last autumn. I woke up on the morning of his death to the old church bell tolling, sounding clearly throughout our quiet community, ringing out a knell for all things simple, pastoral.

After that walk through the first snowy day of our life in the North, we washed all the pears we had gathered earlier, then carefully packed them for the winter in boxes of straw.

Snow melted. A few weeks of Indian summer followed. Often I wandered aimlessly, a little drugged, not knowing exactly what to do or think or feel, soaking up air, smells, countryside, feeling weather and temperature in my bones, filing scenery and wildlife in a memory bank for *my* future generations to enjoy. I bought a bicycle, fitting the back with a kiddie seat, and began pedaling along Ranchitos Road in the afternoons. If I was nervous, that slow-motion tripping calmed me down. From time to time I grew so sleepy, pedaling aimlessly, that I would close my eyes and drift blindly along the deserted road, the sun hot against my face and shoulders: I listened to the sound of wind, faraway sheep bells, a chattering kingfisher.

For fun I might carry a transistor radio in my basket, tuned to the local station, KKIT. I coasted along listening to faint strains of Spanish ranchera music from the afternoon platter show of Judge Norbert Martínez. A midafternoon sunshine pacified the valley. Dogs sprawled in their dusty yards couldn't rouse themselves to charge me snarling. Cattle eyed me with ridiculous bovine stupidity. Only the eyes of horses followed me; they never turned their heads. I savored the tranquillity, often laughing for joy over my pure and irresponsible inactivities. It was like gliding through cream: my whole body was infused with a low-key near orgasm as I goofily propelled that bicycle along Ranchitos Road.

I had a camera and binoculars. After supper Luke and I pedaled two miles down the road, halting when we saw an old-fashioned hay wagon with slatted sides and soft rubber wheels crossing a field. Two massive white work horses pulled the wagon: they were silhouetted against Taos Mountain, on which vibrant russet sunlight lingered. Later we photographed a horse grazing in darkness, only several highlights visible on its flanks and along its neck. Behind the animal another of those enormous clouds, whose undersides were dissolving, let fall pink cotton-candy rain wisps reaching halfway to the mesa. To the west a black almond-shaped cloud, isolated in an otherwise clear sky, had a fiery magenta rim.

Riding home, I kept up a chatter with Luke, calling his attention to bats, to a little camposanto near a corral in which three mangy buffaloes grunted. At a favorite overhang, I stopped and looked down on a prairie-dog village of several dozen families. But by then Luke was sound asleep, tilted half out of his kiddie chair, his mouth wide open, his little fists clenched in his groin, snoring loudly.

On other bike rides we saw silvery turquoise bluebirds, white-crowned sparrows and chipping sparrows, or flocks of migrating Audubon warblers. The countryside was sunny, cottonwoods a warm and buttery yellow, fields beige, irrigation ditches full to overflowing and icy green.

A sudden moment of terror occurred as two hot-rodders, one in an old black Ford pickup, the other in a big-finned ancient Chrysler, came skidding and whining around a curve. Side by side, they accelerated toward us, dragging each other, forcing us into a ditch. By in a gun blast, they fishtailed around the curve ahead, and were gone. But we could hear them for miles, careening around the curve a half mile away by Otto Pitcher's aspen grove near Los Córdovas, and then racing up past the little Los Córdovas church and the boggy fields of Cordillera.

At the mesa above Frances Martin's house we stopped, dismounted, and sat down overlooking the prairie-dog village, the valley beyond. Clouds hugged the mountains, a dove-gray mood to it all. Cottonwoods were yellow, cattle were black against dying fields. Everywhere, new pyramids of hay bales had been stacked near barns: the air was cold and cedar sharp. A snipe flew by. A red-tailed hawk perched high in a dead cottonwood—we stared at it: the bird seemed not to notice us at all. Below, behind Frances Martin's large adobe house, her two white horses strolled by the edge of a small pond, reflected cleanly in the still water.

I eased up,
and just let it happen,
very grateful.

My fishing career began on a picnic beside the Pueblo River about a half mile before it empties into the Rio Grande. Two local old men using fly rods came upstream flicking artificial pieces of fluff expertly into the crannies and crevices of the stream, dropping the lures into foamy corners, dancing them coyly across all shadows and along currents defining rocks both great and small. Fascinated, I observed the approach of these two grizzled viejitos, amazed by the dexterity and finesse with which they handled those fly rods.

Also, as they drew closer, I noticed one man had a footlong brown trout jammed headfirst into his front shirt pocket, three quarters of its rubbery body bent over and jouncing provocatively at every step.

Right then and there I decided that if I did nothing else in Taos for the next ten years, I would sure as hell learn how to be a fisherman!

Early one November morning perhaps a week after this incident, I awoke at seven, staggered out to the chicken coop, broke the watering can ice, and threw wheat, lay pellets, and oyster shells on the leafy ground. Back inside I ate an enormous breakfast of sausage and eggs, then loaded binoculars, a new fishing reel, hooks, salmon eggs, and some sandwiches in my bicycle basket, tied an air pump, a fishing net, and a new rod to the kiddie seat, and hit the road, aiming for the Little Rio Grande beyond Talpa on the Las Vegas highway, about ten miles away. Though bright and sunny, the morning was cold: white frost covered the fields. All along Ranchitos Road kids hung around rural route mailboxes, awaiting school buses. I could barely make out Frances Martin's two white horses against the chilled fields: squinting, the only way to tell of their presence was from the big steamy plumes of their breathing.

I came onto the highway near the Old Martínez Hall, the Ranchos post office, the famous Ranchos church. Pedaling up past the Trading Post, I veered east onto Route 3. Already, frost was melting off Talpa fields. I chugged along slowly, heart beating hard now, sweating a lot, my face beet red. Kids walking to the Talpa elementary called me names; I grinned stupidly and kept pedaling. About a mile beyond the little schoolhouse, I glided down a hill past the last valley alfalfa field, turned a corner, and arrived at the National Forest Boundary. Pulling off the road, I assembled my rod and

Ant hill on western mesa

*Roots and plants near
Hopewell Lake*

trudged a few steps through thick willows into the Little Rio Grande.

For a river that never runs more than a few yards from a section of the major roadway to Las Vegas between Talpa and the Pot Creek lumber mill at the base of U.S. Hill, that stretch of the Little Rio Grande is one hell of a trout stream, even though rarely more than ten feet wide and but a few feet deep. Beginning where I commenced that day, the stream is almost impossible to fish from the bank because of impenetrable willow thickets. Even walking up the middle of the stream, for about two miles overhanging trees and brush make casting a fly nearly impossible. At its worst, the river is masochistic trout fishing at its best. At its best, thanks to the inaccessible water, the stream here is always full of fish. Farther east, the willows thin away and beavers take over. The stream widens into large ponds inundating entire meadows. Then, near the western boundary of Southern Methodist University's Fort Burgwin Research Center, the river meanders out in the open like a small, classic trout stream, an area I almost never visit because it is too accessible, very popular, often fished out of brown trout, and stocked regularly with untasty hatchery rainbows that fall easy prey to bait fishermen.

Don't get me wrong: I'm no snob about bait. I don't even know how to use bait, and often wish I did when down on a river like the Rio Grande, getting skunked on flies. But I don't enjoy eating the fish that much, and I love the sport involved in flies — it has simply become my way over the years, that's all.

In the beginning, however, I had no confidence I could lure a trout onto an artificial fly. Approaching the Little Rio Grande that November day eight years ago, all I had in mind was catching a fish. If I'd had some, I probably would have tossed dynamite into the river! Or, following a recipe given to me by my Ranchitos neighbor Bernardo Trujillo, I might have lugged a cider jug out there, dropped in a chunk of raw lime, poured water on the lime and capped the bottle tightly, dropped it into the water as the gassy reaction built up, and blown those trout sky high using materials considerably cheaper, and much more legal, than TNT.

Where I entered the willows, the stream was not wide Channels were a foot, two feet deep, the riffles shallow inches of fast water. In many places, willow thickets made it impossi-

ble to approach the water by land. Here and there patches of dying grass hung over the bank, trailing long dead filaments in the water, perfect protection for trout. Large shady junipers grew at regular intervals along the stream. A few small beaver dams had forged marshy flooded areas. Rocky, covered with piñon trees, mountain foothills rose up almost immediately from the southern bank. And occasionally rabbit brush as tall as my head lined the riverside.

With luck, I thought I might catch a fish. Baiting up a size 8 snelled hook with a couple of fireballs (the idea of it *now* makes me ashamed!), I drifted the bait under the bank, immediately had a strike, and one second later hauled a thirteen-inch brown trout onto the bank. Unhooking it, I banged the fish dead against a rock, wrapped it in damp grass, and, somewhat stunned, baited up my hook again.

On my first fishing expedition in northern New Mexico it had taken me approximately seven seconds to land my initial trout!

Farther on I had an interesting duel with a hatchery rainbow. The fish rose, taking the bait almost as soon as it entered the water. I struck, it escaped. I spent five minutes untangling my line from a thicket overhanging the stream, affixed more eggs, and lowered them in. The same fish rose and gobbled — I struck, and spent another five minutes unsnarling line. The same procedure followed, I drifted the bait into the water, and my fish sucked in the iridescent caviar: I yanked so hard this time around that I spent a full ten minutes disentangling my line from the willows and vines surrounding me. If the fish kept hitting, I was perfectly willing to feed it bait, however, so I tried again. Only this time I let it swallow the bait, digest it, and just about defecate before striking — and landed my second New Mexico trout, born and bred in the Red River (Taos County) Hatchery, no doubt: but us beggars weren't about to be choosy.

Pushing on, I caught two more little browns, stashing them in my shirt pockets, of course. This fishing was sweets from the kiddies! Around noon, though, when I backtracked along the stream, I couldn't locate my big trout. Carefully wrapped in grass, the fish had disappeared into the foliage. I couldn't believe it, how could I have been so stupid? This was my *trophy!* And we are talking, here, about a meat hunter from way Way Back! I doubled up on my trail, crawling on hands and knees, desperate to locate that precious brown. I actually began to panic, cursing the river, the fish, my lunatic idiocy. Then quite by accident I stepped on the thing, perfectly camouflaged in a clump of grass similar to its wrapping.

Snapping off scallops of ice from roots drooping into the river, I wrapped my fish carefully in grass and leaves, the ice against their smooth flanks, and set the bundle tenderly in the bicycle basket. Believe me, as I pedaled out of there, just by closing my eyes for a second I could picture the Irati River outside Pamplona, Spain.

They were very good fish, and I had caught them truly, and I felt very happy!

Eight years later, my passion for trout fishing has not diminished. Having become a semi-able craftsman with the fly line, I like to fish areas that offer some room for maneuvering. And as I grow older, I find it no longer an attractive proposition to spend five hours duck-waddling up a damp tunnel in order to catch slightly more than a half dozen eight-inch trout. Recently I have spent much time on the Rio Grande where the water is deep, the fish can be enormous, and the banks are unobstructed. Yet I will always remain true to the little streams where I began, southwest of Taos, commencing only twenty minutes from my front door: the Rio Chiquito, Pot Creek, and the Little Rio Grande.

Only yesterday, immediately after writing the above, I couldn't stop myself from returning to the exact area I had described. It hasn't changed much in eight years, except the highway parking area was badly trashed with garbage: the stream was murky from spring runoff. Using size 12 Rio Grande Kings, almost instantly I began to get bites. But they spit out the fly as fast as they took it, and I struck too soon, too late, too hard, too soft. Bitterly, I blundered awkwardly through thickets even more impenetrable than they had been years ago. Nowhere could I maneuver for a halfway decent roll cast, let alone the real thing. Yet every time I managed to drop, roll, or snap a fly onto the water without causing a disturbance, a little trout lunged at it and was instantly gone.

In two hours I had thirty-seven strikes, and landed but six fish.

One of my boots, punctured by a beaver-manufactured punji stick, had filled up with water early — and now I also have a bad cold.

Likewise, typing is painful because my fingertips are rife with minute thorns.

But I loved those six little trout. I can't begin to tell you how much more a trout can be enjoyed if the taking of it involves almost all-out guerrilla warfare, coupled with sensationally delicate finesse, and nothing short of Marine-inspired survival training is needed to bag the beautiful little bastard!

Nearly as often as we fetched wood that autumn, I went fishing. Having no confidence in flies, I used salmon eggs and worms almost exclusively because what I needed right then was to bag trout . . . put 'em on the table . . . be able to exhibit the fruits of my meanderings.

Later I would worry about art.

Mostly I fished up east of Questa, high on the Red River, a stream I never touch now, an area I dislike intensely. Not long ago, Red River was a farming town. Today it is entirely oriented toward tourism and recreation. There is not a single Spanish surname in the Red River phone directory. A ski area, motorcycle rental shops, and other businesses are all concerned with summer and winter leisure activities. It's a Texas town, and seems completely alien to the rhythm of the rest of this land.

In summertime, fishing the stretch of river where I began in earnest to chase down trout requires little skill. At regular intervals Fish and Game trucks dump in hundreds of ten- to twelve-inch-long rainbow trout. And, although I don't believe there is a recreation director who actually blows a whistle, what occurs immediately after the fish plant resembles my concept of an Oklahoma land rush.

The fish hit the river, and within seconds wall-to-wall tourists are going after them with everything from marshmallow balls to double-edged axes. The fish themselves seem to have been cleverly starved for a week, hence they'll bite at anything that lands in the water. For a day or two the Red River resembles an abattoir, as all kinds of fisherpeople catch, club, grab, stomp, shoot, and loot anything in the water vaguely resembling a trout. Then it's over. And, in the same sad way western prairies were once littered with buffalo guts and bones, the shores of the Red River hum with the buzzing

Sunset from Padre Martínez home, Taos

Tres Orejas Mountain, Carson Mesa

of a trillion flies lunching on miles of piles of trout guts and other assorted indignities.

But in November and December, when I first learned to fish, nobody else plied the river, and it was beautiful. Steller's jays, nuthatches, and chickadees cavorted in the tall pine trees along the bank; often little chipmunks chattered incessantly. Snow covered the ground; sometimes it fell quietly as I worked the stream. The air was cold. Every few minutes my rod ferrules iced up and I had to stop, chipping off the ice. On some late-November days the weather was so cold I had to pause every few minutes, jamming my hands into my crotch for warmth.

But the serenity of fishing in ice and snow is so attractive I have become an inveterate bad-weather angler. No experience is better than pulling a rainbow trout from gloomy, lead-green water during a thick snowfall on a windless day, and laying that silver-and-pink body on clean white powder in the shadow of a thick spruce tree.

Almost always a chunky gray dipper bird (a water ouzel) joined me right at the start of my day, and stayed with me, advancing along one pool ahead, without ever disturbing the trout. Probably at least a third of the time that I fish in small streams in this county, I am joined by one of these cheerful underwater scavengers, who stays with me for hours, always just one pool ahead of my pace. In a curious way, I have come to depend on their companionship.

With a handful of trout in my jacket pockets after fishing the Red River, I drove into Questa and stopped at Louie's Café for coffee or hot chocolate, a slice of cherry pie. I always shot a coin in the jukebox, playing the latest Tammy Wynette or Jerry Lee Lewis song, and sat in the warm glow of that quiet café feeling dreamy and warm, wishing I could just stay like that forever. And no moments in my life have given more pleasure than those restful times in Louie's Café after my cold weather days on the Red River, my body numb and all tuckered out, imbued with an almost orgasmic fatigue.

On a bright summer day I am alone high on the Rio Chiquito, a stream barely as wide as I am tall. The scent of wild mint makes the air pungent: raspberry bushes full of ripe red fruit line the river, and I stop often to pluck juicy handfuls. Legions of hummingbirds are feeding at veins of scarlet penstemon running through the high meadows around me. There are butterflies galore: painted ladies, yellow swallowtails, tortoise shells, Weidemeyer's admirals, angle-wings, fritillaries. A duck and three ducklings sputter frantically across a pool ahead of me; an Oregon junco and two of its young nervously assess me from a streamside bush. In muddy places, on slim little sandbars, I spot many deer tracks. I move along easily on this quiet, exquisite day, constantly pumping my fly rod, using a black badger fly, wet, or a little Joe's hopper, fished dry, and drawing a strike from almost every pool. I'm keeping a diary of this day's angling, and around four o'clock, when I decide to quit, I add up the score. In all, I have had fifty-five strikes. I have kept ten fish, eight to eleven inches long, eight browns and two native cutthroats, and I have caught twenty-two other fish, which I returned to the river.

The incredible richness of trout-fishing these streams and lakes near my home often leaves me almost speechless. For example: a friend from Philadelphia, Mike Kimmel, and I are heading up to the high mountain lakes for the first time. Shortly after dawn we approach Heart Lake, five miles above Cabresto Lake, near Questa. We have brought little food and are counting on trout to keep us well fed over the next three days. Cautiously, then, we approach the lake on our hands and knees. Streams of mist curl across the placid water. In mountain saddles above us, patches of snow shine mysteriously. A marmot whistles; picas are chattering. Taking forever, we carefully set up our rods, suck in deep breaths, and cast onto the quiet water. Before either of us can utter an exclamation, we have tied into vigorously jumping trout. Three minutes later we've accumulated a dozen little cutthroats for a lavish breakfast. After the feast, arrogantly smoking his pipe, stripped to the nude in order to soak up the bennies, Mike lazily stands at the edge of the lake catching a trout with each cast, releasing it, and catching another one with his next cast.

On a different occasion, Mike and I climb up to the nine Latir Lakes, located in Taos County close to the Colorado border. It is evening when we arrive at the highest lake, and there seems to be nothing doing. The water is calm, no fish are rising. On the precipitous mountain slopes towering above the southern shore, sheep are grazing. I sit by the water's edge, peering into the depths, searching for signs of life. Suddenly I notice a beast that resembles a submarine! Moments later I see an enormous fish rise and, with a tiny sucking *thup!* that barely causes a ripple, it takes in a minuscule bug. Within seconds I've dropped a size 18 dry mosquito close to that spot, and immediately, following another barely perceptible *thup!*, I've hooked a heavy fifteen-inch cutthroat.

In the next hour before dark, alone on this twelve-thousand-foot-high body of water, we land seven such fish that we will talk about for the rest of our lives.

It is at the Latirs that I see my first water shrew, a tiny animal that swims on the surface out from the bank, dives suddenly, roots about on the bottom, locating a grub, swims back to the surface, and returns to the bank barely two feet away from my nose.

Other animals that abound up there are the bushy-tailed marmots and little fuzzy gray picas that remind me of miniature koala bears. Noisy black and white Clark's nutcrackers swarm in the pine tops, sounding to me like jackdaws. Tiny least weasels inhabit the rocks. And once a large coyote trotted nonchalantly across a high meadow, oblivious to us onlookers.

It is also in that high country, one October, that I have my first experience with bears.

Hiking into Heart Lake alone, I unroll my goose-down sleeping bag in a sheltered area under a thick pine tree. The foot-deep snow surrounding the lake has been trampled by bears. So many fresh tracks abound that I wonder if there's been some sort of ursine convention recently. The presence of these large animals—who should have been asleep by now—assures that I'll be awake all night, a spoon and a frying pan beside my head as noisemakers to ward them off if they should dare approach my encampment.

Just before dark I glance up, and, against the deepening turquoise sky on a ridge high above me, I see silhouetted a large buck deer and his doe.

The following morning I climb over the saddle leading to the Latirs. Five hundred feet above the fourth lake, I pause atop a steep talus slope that is now a half-mile snowy slide. There's a temptation to sit down and skid all the way to the frozen lake, but I am alone, and suppose I broke a leg—? Yet in thinking back, I wish now that I had had the guts to do it.

Sometimes the high country is a prolific provider; on other occasions it plays me for the fool. Early one autumn, after waiting all summer for the opportunity to take a vacation, a girl friend and I hike into Bear Lake, then the southernmost body of water in the Wheeler Peak Wilderness Area. More recently, the lake has been turned over to the Taos Pueblo by the Department of the Interior. Breathtakingly beautiful, Bear Lake is a nearly square, deeply turquoise alpine pond surrounded on three sides by steeply rising pine forests and talus slopes. So many rainbow trout are dimpling that it seems as if rain is falling. We set up camp, catch several trout for supper . . . and then the parade begins. It starts with a half dozen Forest Service personnel toting rifles and walkie-talkies: they tromp past our dinner fire and set up camp in the trees nearby. Next, a helicopter flies into the sierra bowl and lands on a ridge above us, rotors whirring, lights blinking. Finally, come dark, while we are eating our fish, ten men from the Pueblo suddenly march through our campsite. Their leader, Paul Bernal, halts, and, very politely, he says, "Nice to see you in the wilderness."

Wilderness? For the next two days we will hear nothing but rifle shots, walkie-talkies, and the deafening roar of the circling helicopter. The Taos Indians have recently won back their sacred Blue Lake land, and apparently all this activity is an attempt to locate ancient surveying boundary markers.

At dusk, when things have settled a bit, my friend and I try a little peaceful fly casting. The air is rife with tiny, swooping bats. Sometimes they fly so close to my head that I flinch. Then I hear a *whack!* followed by a splash: "I just knocked a bat into the water with my rod!" my friend exclaims. A moment later I do exactly the same thing, belting a bat out into the water forty feet away while I'm casting. Apparently used to such indignities, the bat swims to shore like a Johnny Weissmuller, rests for a while on a log licking itself, and then takes off.

Next year, when Mike and I hike into Bear Lake, the hex is still on. This time it proves impossible to catch a trout. Perched on the bank, we can see thousands of fish cruising back and forth through the crystal water: it's almost like standing on the edge of a hatchery pond! Not only that, but they are feeding constantly: again the dimples of rising trout make it appear that a steady rain is falling. But they won't take anything we have to offer. We start with tiny dry flies: adams and

Hopewell Lake high country an hour west of Taos

Snowstorm lifting off Ranchos—Llano Quemado Valley

mosquitoes and irresistibles. After that we fling every pattern in the book at them — dry, wet, you name it. The fish pay no attention. We work our fly rods, then change to spinning rods, using wet flies and plastic bubbles. Nothing. So we switch to hardware, going through Colorado spinners, Panther Martins, Mepps, and using every retrieve possible — no dice. Finally, we hunt for worms, gather a canful, and try that. A freak accident happens — Mike lands a ten-inch fish on a worm! "The problem is solved!" we cry. But not one more rainbow, over the next two days, bites another worm. And we hike out of there empty-handed, defeated by a lake so full of trout we practically could have walked across the water on their backs!

Shut out today, there's always chance for glory tomorrow. And, as I fish the high country at 12,000 feet, I also sometimes ply the deep gorges, 6,000 feet closer to sea level. In the Wild River section of the Rio Grande, near Questa where the Red River enters the larger artery, white water cascades between enormous boulders. I cast a Panther Martin spinner across the river, and, while retrieving it quickly, a big rainbow hits and is over a waterfall before I know exactly what has happened. Racing for my life, and my prize, I scramble downstream over boulders, and through white water, almost dropping my rod, nearly killing myself, trying to follow that fish. Five minutes of combat ensue: then, in a toss-up of who's more exhausted, me or it, I land the eighteen-inch trout and let out a triumphant yell: can the twenty-inch barrier hold up for long — ?

Closer to home, I discover that the Rio Grande near Arroyo Hondo, twenty minutes from my door, provides good autumn brown-trout fishing. The river is low and clear, and the first time, following a friend's tip, that I land on this section of the big river, I can't believe my eyes. Everywhere, trout are jumping. Not just ten-, twelve-, fifteen-inch trout: some of these lunkers are enormous! They bolt out of the water like shots, their momentum carrying them sometimes two feet or more above the surface, where they turn sideways, and slap back down loudly against the river. Flies they won't touch, so I immediately switch to spinners. One evening I land two browns measuring eleven and thirteen inches, and three more tipping the ruler at fourteen and fifteen inches. The following day I land more of the same. But the enormous lunkers keep jumping, tantalizing me, urging me on. For two weeks I fish that section of the river every day after work, hoping for a Moby Trout. I land more trout poundage than I ever have before, but I still can't nail one of those lunkers that look like salmon jumping.

At night, as I clamber back down the river over boulders, trying to avoid the cholla cactuses that lie in wait for my unsuspecting hands to grab, the echoing hoots of owls high up in the cliff walls seem to mock my inability to land a big one.

One day I carry home three sixteen-inch trout, one fifteen-incher, and one thirteen-incher. But it's getting cold; the lunkers have gone under; we are into December . . . and after that the fish are leaping no more. Sadly, I decide I'm not going to land a behemoth, not this year anyway.

But Christmas Day dawns bright, overly warm, and sunny. I am alone for the holiday, and so I decide to give the river another shot. The water is low and clear from lack of snow and rainfall: the gorge and the Rio Grande are deserted. I see the tracks of both a mountain lion and a bobcat in mud along the banks. Kingfishers are chattering up and down the canyon. Mallards, buffleheads, and two mergansers fly past me. There is no wind on the river. I come to a sandbank where I can see the skid marks of playful otters sliding into the river: twice I almost stepped on these animals when they surfaced near me.

Despite the sunshine, the water is cold, the trout aren't moving, I get no hits for a while. Then, around one o'clock, fishing a black-and-white Dardevle as close to the bottom as I can get it, I feel a strike, set the hook, and commence a ten-minute battle with a sluggish but powerful fish. When I ease it onto the sandbar where I'm standing, it turns out to be the longest trout that I've ever landed: a nineteen-inch rainbow.

But the twenty-inch barrier looks safe for another season.

Sometimes these adventures in search of trout are made more poignant by the fact that such experiences may become rare during my lifetime. I seem to be living at the heart of one of the last wild sections of our country, one of the least populated (and publicized) natural regions. Yet all the portents of doom that abound elsewhere are firmly rooted here also. I remember a day several years ago when a small incident seems terribly significant. I have been at Williams Lake, in the Wheeler Peak Wilderness Area near Taos Ski Valley, but decide to leave early because the lake is so crowded with campers it's more like Coney Island than a wilderness setting. Walking back, I pass onto private land where the Taos Ski Valley is expanding its operations, cutting up a fresh mountainside, installing new chair lifts. The air is shattered regularly with shock waves from dynamite blasting: bulldozers, heaps of earth, and downed trees clutter the picturesque little valley at the foot of a chair lift.

Thirsty from the hike, I approach a tiny stream, barely three feet wide, that meanders through the valley. Kneeling to drink, I notice a flickering shape in the water. Pausing, I realize I'm looking at a seven-inch trout. Carefully, I withdraw. Using a dozen rocks, at the bottom of the shallow pool I make a dam to trap the fish. Then I reach down and slowly close my fingers around the trout — it doesn't move as I grasp, lifting it from the water . . . a lovely native fish, one of the last of the Rio Grande cutthroats, which have been nearly rubbed out these past decades by poor timbering practices, recreation development, and proliferating brown trout.

I keep the fish, seeing no future for it in this bulldozed valley, and eat it that night, almost ceremonially, wondering if I am ever going to see another of these endangered little trout again. They exist today high on the Rio Chiquito, Pot Creek, and the Little Rio Grande. Each summer I land one or two on flies. But they are almost extinct.

It is like a sweet dream for me, this pursuit of trout. I see myself on an April evening, moving up a tiny river. The afternoon has been warm: it is turning chill now, a truly quiet evening. For a moment, the fish are surface-feeding. Crouched over, literally duck-waddling, I approach a wide smooth pool narrowing into a quick riffle down at my end. Up at the head of the pool two trout are jumping. I take my time, blowing on my fly to dry it out so that it will float. Then, in this early-spring dusk, with the air suddenly brisk and the trout still feeding, before I can cast, snowflakes begin to fall. I stop, looking up at the sky which was clear only a moment ago. Then I false-cast a few times and drop my fly just below the feeding fish: immediately there's a hit. I strike too hard, and the trout is lifted out of the water. It's still hanging in the air as the fly snaps back and bounces off my nose. Then the fish returns to the water with a slim splash, and suddenly the little pool that was so active seconds ago is quiet . . . but for the easy snow falling and the darkness coming on.

And I sit there, dreamy and tired and strangely ecstatic, wishing I could live forever.

Absorbed in a physical life, spending much of my time outdoors, I hadn't been reading during the late summer and autumn of that year. But as cold weather quieted down the valley, I spent more time indoors, and got into books again. The first task I set for myself was to learn at least an outline history of the land around me. From the Harwood Library I checked out a dozen volumes related to Taos and, in a week or so, acquired a surface knowledge of the history invisibly pulsing through the picturesque valley.

The Taos Pueblo was founded around 1200 A.D. Several centuries later, in 1540, Coronado's officer Hernando Alvarado became the first white man officially to visit Taos. In 1598, shortly after he established a settlement downriver in Española, Don Juan de Oñate arrived in the area. Missionaries, taxes, and a general repression of the Pueblo people followed. In 1631, Taos tribe members murdered a padre and two soldiers. Relentlessly, conquering Spaniards forced native peoples into a slave-labor existence: Indians worked in local mines under terrible conditions, they lugged enormous timbers and heavy stones to build churches that would help eradicate their own religion. By 1680, the local folk had had enough. Led by a San Juan Pueblo man named Popé, Taos natives joined a revolt and marched on Santa Fe, rubbing out every Spaniard that got in the way, and forging a final sixteen years of freedom before the Spaniards returned for good. After 1696, when Father Antonio Carbonel became the town's fourth and final padre martyr, the Spanish were never headed again.

Taos village grew up some five miles south of the Pueblo. Eastern Plains Indians, notably Comanches, made life hard for all valley residents, alternately trading with and massacring the Pueblo Indians or more recent settlers. Defying Mexican laws, French fur traders invaded the southern Rockies, exacerbating tensions in the area. In 1761 Comanches killed or carried away some fifty Spanish-surnamed women and children. A year later, Santa Fe soldiers, led by Manuel Partillo Urrisola, killed four hundred Comanches in a single Taos Valley battle, and things calmed down for a while.

By the early 1800s, American traders had started moving into what is now northern New Mexico. Taos became an important waypost in the profitable overland trade between the United States and Mexico. For a while it reigned as the capital

The mountain as seen from Lower Ranchitos

Near Shady Brook, Taos Canyon

of the southwest fur trade. Bautiste LaLande was the first American trader to hit town. A number of famous trappers followed, among them Ewing Young, William Wolfskill, and Luis Robidoux. Within two decades Taos had become a haven for many famous mountain men. Kit Carson arrived in 1826, making his home base in Taos: four decades later he was buried in a park only a few blocks from his original residence. Dick Wootton, a famous trapper and jack of all transgressions, occasionally rode a white horse into local saloons and shot out the lights. Peg Leg Smith was a noted horse trader of those days. A renowned bear fighter, Jim Baker, moved in and out of the valley according to his needs. Ceran St. Vrain, a St. Louis trapper, merchant, and soldier, established a store in Taos with Charles Bent: both men often rode at the head of wagon trains bringing supplies to their Taos establishment. Old Bill Williams, noted trapper, guide, and mountain man, once tried storekeeping in Taos, but lost heart with the bureaucracy involved, pitched his stock out the front door, and scrambled back into the mountains. He once served as guide on John C. Frémont's infamous Fourth Expedition, which wound up floundering south along the Rio Grande in bitter winter snows, a disaster comparable to the Sierra Nevada's Donner Party fiasco. Edward and Richard Kern, graphic artists accompanying that doomed expedition, are given credit for being the first artists to visit Taos.

The same year, 1826, that Kit Carson showed up, one of New Mexico's most famous and controversial characters arrived in the valley — the Reverend Antonio José Martínez. Taking over the Catholic parish, he promptly started a school for both boys *and* girls, and launched New Mexico's first printing press, from which, for a short while, he published the territory's initial newspaper, called *El Crepúsculo*. Unlike most of his cohorts, the padre had no stomach for Mexico's unfair tax laws, which hit his congregation hard: he also denounced his own church's abuse of power. The man had studied law and was probably the most learned and progressive figure the territory had ever seen. In 1854, when he refused to collect unfair church taxes, he was defrocked by Bishop Lamy of Santa Fe. The padre promptly built his own church. For years he lived with a common-law wife and had a number of children. He died in 1867.

One controversial aspect of Padre Martínez's life involved his alleged sympathy for the rebellion of 1847. In conjunction with the U.S. occupation of Mexico, General Stephen Watts Kearny had marched his troops down through the northern part of Mexican territory, claiming it all for America. He appointed Charles Bent of Taos first territorial governor and, without firing a shot, proceeded on to California. Several months after his departure, Taos Indians revolted, killing the Taos sheriff, prefect, prosecuting attorney, a judge's son, the brother-in-law of Governor Bent, and Bent himself, who was first scalped alive, then riddled with bullets in front of his own family and Kit Carson's wife. Many more Americans died in the uprising. Then troops marched up from Santa Fe and the real killing began. Joined by Ceran St. Vrain, and such mountain men as Dick Wootton and Jim Beckwourth, the soldiers corralled most of the rebels in the north Pueblo church, proceeded to blow holes in the thick adobe with howitzers, and slaughtered about two hundred natives. A dozen surviving conspirators were summarily tried and hanged in a field north of town.

War continued as a way of life in Taos. In 1854, angry Jicarilla Apaches eradicated some soldiers a half hour south of town, in Embudo. The following year Ceran St. Vrain, among others, fought a short war of extermination against Utes and Jicarillas up in southern Colorado, and that ended that. The Civil War arrived, and mostly bypassed Taos, a town that sided with the North. An act of patriotism in 1861 created a situation giving Taos a lot of tourist mileage today. Irked by the contrary nature of local denizens who kept tearing down the Plaza's American flag, Kit Carson, Captain Smith H. Simpson, and other Yankee sympathizers nailed the flag to a stout cottonwood pole, and kept guard over it night and day, threatening to plug anyone who laid a finger on it. Today, by special act of Congress, the U.S. flag on the Plaza flies twenty-four hours a day in commemoration of that gesture over a century ago.

By the second half of the nineteenth century, people seemed winded from two hundred years of relentless oppression and hostility; organized slaughter petered out. America consolidated her hold on the fledgling territory; a new legal apparatus kept Taos Valley locals backed up against the wall, fighting to hang on to their lands. Then the 1866 discovery of gold in the Moreno Valley a half hour east of Taos changed the nature of exploitation: Elizabethtown became the first mining boom site in the area. By 1890 the hills were like Swiss cheese, full of holes probing into the earth, searching for a rich vein. Men often paid their bills in gold, and one Taos doctor kept delicate troy scales in his office for weighing out the valuable dust. In 1893 the town of Amizett was established in the Hondo Canyon; in 1895, farther up that same canyon where the Taos Ski Valley is located today, a town called Twining was born. It didn't last long. A large smelter that never worked properly was built, christened with much fanfare, and then abandoned overnight. Aside from the active molybdenum mine in Questa, mining has never been that big in the county again. Remnants of the old gold fever are everywhere, however. Once, climbing on my hands and knees up a nearly vertical slope south of Wheeler Peak a dozen miles from any access path, I came across a caved-in mine shaft, and was amazed that the lust for wealth would lead a miner to such a precipitous remote location.

During the heyday of numerous mining ventures, the usual conglomeration of colorful misfits gathered around various fly-by-night endeavors, and the county's history is liberally sprinkled with tall tales of gamblers, bootleggers, prostitutes, murderers, and so forth. Humbuggery clotted the air, cantinas flourished, outlaws glowered threateningly. Americans stealing Spanish land grants hired gun thugs to terrorize angry locals bent on stealing back their stolen territory. A revolutionary society, called the Gorras Blancas, consisted of local men who burned new settlers' corrals and ranchos, cut barbed wire, and rustled cattle, in general making things tough on the American thieves overrunning their territory. Seventy miles east of Taos, a Las Vegas ne'er-do-well named Vicente Silva surrounded himself with notorious bandits and corrupt politicos, and his pandilla wreaked havoc in that wide-open town for a while. Breaking off from that band, twins known as Miguel and Francisco Maes were granted a highwayman dealership in Taos County. Among other depredations, they were credited with hanging an Arroyo Hondo sheepherder named Boy Ramón, who refused to divulge the location of a buried treasure. To the northeast, just beyond the Moreno Valley in Cimarron, Clay Allison, "the Corpse Maker of Colfax County," built a reputation as a "gentleman" killer. When a chief justice issued a warrant for Allison's arrest, three men, including a nephew of Davy Crockett, lost their lives in a hotel shoot-out stemming from the attempt to serve that paper. Allison eventually died ignominiously when he fell from a wagon and a wheel crushed his head.

The Spanish-American War in 1898 further provoked ill feelings between Americans and local citizens. When the Taos sheriff, Luciano Trujillo, was shot to death in an altercation with young Albert Gifford, a new massacre — of Americans — seemed imminent. While angry mobs searched for Gifford, a woman named Lina Scheurich hid the boy in a well. Lacking a leader to focus their anger politically, the mob cooled off: and no revolution, or systematic genocide, occurred.

Eight years later Teddy Roosevelt pulled off the biggest Taos County land grab ever by incorporating many of the Southwest's communal lands into a National Forest system. Almost half of Taos County, including the Pueblo's sacred Blue Lake terrain, passed into federal jurisdiction, laying a bitter groundwork for battles, such as the Tierra Amarilla courthouse raid, that would take place in the North sixty years later.

As I plowed through one book after another during the early winter of 1969, it became increasingly difficult to separate the grit from the gristle in Taos history. The valley was always chock-full of tall-tale tellers and theatrical braggarts, and the myths and legends growing out of its wide-open days are a dime a dozen. So many colorful characters moved into town that the historical set for a while resembled the landscape of a Robert Altman movie. One truly blue-blooded rascal to set up shop during the latter part of the nineteenth century was Long John Dunn, a cardsharp, gunfighter, barkeep, elk hunter, etc., ad infinitum. He built a toll bridge over the Rio Grande at Arroyo Hondo, and made a fortune transporting passengers from the La Servilleta railroad station to Taos in stagecoaches. Later he owned the first car in Taos: and was subsequently wiped out when highways were laid down and made navigable.

Another famous Taos story concerns an Englishman, one Arthur Manby, who for many years applied his megalomaniacal hand to the area, attempting to gather up all the land in sight, establishing an empire of note. Instead, he was found beheaded one day in 1929: or anyway, a body purporting to be his, whose head had been chewed off by dogs, was discovered in his house. To this day much mystery, in-

The world below Justin Locke's house

The Valdez Valley, north of Taos

cluding a hundred tales of buried treasure and grisly murderous acts, surround that mysterious imperialist.

The currently famous, or infamous, Taos Art Colony dates itself back, officially, to 1898, when Bert G. Phillips settled in town and sent out the word that began a stampede. Commencing in the early 1900s, many fairly noted artists appeared in the valley and planted esoteric roots. By the mid-twenties Taos was cluttered with palettes and berets. Henry Sharp, Ernest L. Blumenschein, Oscar E. Berninghaus, Nicolai Fechin, and Leon Gaspard are names which can cause surviving old-timers to draw a hallowed breath. One day the notorious Mabel Dodge arrived, married a Pueblo man called Tony Lujan, and established a salon which catered to the likes of Georgia O'Keeffe, Edward Arlington Robinson, John Marin, Jean Toomer, and Thomas Wolfe. Edward Weston dropped by and took photographs; Willa Cather spent the summer of 1925 with Mabel Dodge. The most notorious visitor was D. H. Lawrence: though he spent but a handful of months in northern New Mexico, his presence dominates its aesthetic and scandal-oriented legacies. Frieda Lawrence and Dorothy Brett are household names in the valley: and those few months of the novelist's stay engendered enough apocryphal stories to last a millennium! After Lawrence died, Frieda returned to Taos with his ashes, which are entombed in a tiny shrine north of town. And that shrine, the Pueblo, the Taos Ski Valley, and Kit Carson's memory seem to be the four hard diamonds upon which current hysterical tourist operations are founded. . . .

So it was, becoming acclimated to my first high-country winter, that I learned something about the dramatic nature of the times that had forged the turbulent and beautiful Taos Valley, giving such a theatrical luster to its present-day life.

Over the winter, hemmed in, things changed. We had been drifting with the seasons, working hard physically, seeking relief from New York City by gathering wood, fishing, taking long bike rides, moving around on the land. Yet though grateful for the rustic break, we were, underneath, uneasy. Because life went on outside. And once you feel connected to worldwide historical processes, there's no solace in a solitary, self-indulgent life. I feel uncomfortable if I cannot read a newspaper every day, continually reaffirming my social and political connections. And by the time winter settled, new juices were flowing. Having learned some natural laws governing survival in this country, we began re-establishing other rhythms from our New York days. An anti–Vietnamese War moratorium committee had formed in town, and we joined. A disproportionate number of Raza men from Taos County were being drafted for Southeast Asia and killed over there. An anti-war senator who later became New Mexico's attorney general was invited to talk, and I became publicity chairman. We made posters, tracked down duplicators for leaflets, put ads in the local paper, asked stores to display our posters. On chill wintry afternoons I traipsed from one end of town to the other, fitting leaflets under car windshield wipers.

Then Ruby decided to visit Cuba on a Venceremos Brigade, and, three months pregnant, she settled into a routine of studying about the island, preparing for her trip.

The pace of our lives changed: the telephone started ringing often. In my writing I always seemed to be playing catch-up, working late into the night, sleeping little. January of 1970 began the fifth straight year in which I failed to write a novel the publishers would accept. Thank God I couldn't foresee that three more years would pass before I finally had a third novel accepted! I was frightened, and had started wondering about my floundering career.

Water left in the front ditch froze solid. One day I donned my hockey skates and stroked along the narrow acequia on our property, then climbed the fence and traveled several hundred yards along Tom Trujillo's ditch, south toward Sebastian's Bar. The channel was only a few feet wide, and I had to stroke-hop-and-sidestep nimbly to avoid air pockets. But it was fun. Just the idea of Hans Brinker in scruffy northern New Mexico left me exhilarated!

Not more than a year later I would start playing hockey in deadly earnest for the first time since college, when my writing for a muckraking paper threw me together with a guy named Em Hall. Em was — still is, for that matter — a gangly, snaggle-toothed, frowzy-haired preppie, writer, lawyer, Renaissance bum from New Canaan, Connecticut, an emotional and intellectual disaster case indubitably one of the better investigative journalists and water-law whizzes around, another of the walking wounded who has since retired to a subsistence existence of legal scuffles, and trout fishing, over in Pecos.

Em also is, or at least was before his last car accident, the best hockey player in New Mexico.

For a couple of years, during the early seventies, Em and I played together in a three-team Albuquerque amateur hockey league. We had uniforms; they played "The Star-Spangled Banner" before our games; a league statistician phoned all contest results into the Albuquerque *Journal*, and delivered a mimeographed stat sheet to each player every two weeks. Comprised of alcoholic ex-Canadian players, Good Old Air Force Boys and other military hatchet men, and elite over-the-hill eastern college players like Em and I (Princeton, Hamilton), the league also fronted a bunch of beefy young Albuquerque boys brought up in the local peewee system, who could skate like hell, lacked hockey savvy, and, resenting the crafty old jokers twice their age, enjoyed maiming us.

It was the goddamnedest, head-huntingest, most hatchet-wielding, spear-chucking little raggle-taggle hockey experience I ever indulged in — but it was fun. I commuted three hours down from Taos, and three hours back home, all in the same day, twice a week during the season, in order to spend an hour and a half on the ice with a bunch of maniacs intent on dismembering my aging body. I usually picked Em up in Santa Fe and we drove down to Iceland — Burque's Roman Coliseum — together.

We played together. And engaged in a melee about once every six minutes together too. We scored goals together; and sat out major misconduct penalties together. We even vomited together after the games.

But we survived; and the experience went with the style of our muckraking newspaper, and with northern New Mexico.

The drives back, after I had dropped Em off in Santa Fe, were for me often the most beautiful part of the experience. Those lonely winter nights were intensified by my fatigue and the danger of sudden weather changes. So exhausted I felt euphoric, I would head up the deserted highway at 2 a.m. on a bright full-moon night with the outside temperature steady at ten below zero, and the numerous stars as bright as summer daisies. Sometimes I turned off the lights, zooming through empty Velarde into the gorge, taking the perilous twisting curves as fast as I could, singing jubilantly at the top of my voice, almost hallucinating from fatigue, as high as I've ever been on life. On other, warmer nights, I often traveled through snowstorms in the dark gorge, stopping to put on chains at the Embudo hospital turnoff, and then praying aloud for divine help as I chugged slowly up the steep slick road beyond Pilar, straining to achieve the top of the gorge and Taos mesa. Halfway up that grueling final hill, I twice met deer on the road, small bunches of four or five animals curiously giving me the eye. Unwilling to stop for fear of losing momentum, I leaned on the horn, cursing those lovely animals, heading straight for them. Only at the very last moment would they suddenly dissolve unconcernedly, melting mirage-like into the storm. At home, I stood in the back field, feeling that acre of clean space around me — sore, bruised, very happy. Inside, taking a 3 a.m. bath, soaking luxuriously in the hot tub, I felt vibrant and alive, ecstatically doomed to eternal youth —

Now, those glory days are over. Last winter, Em and I descended on the Los Alamos rink a few times, nuking those arrogant physicists with our fast-fading twine-denting talents. But by and large, the roar of the rabid crowd is forever behind us. Em has settled into the bucolic life-and-death malaria-ridden struggle to survive in rustic Pecos, where he's learned local Spanish to the extent he can barely speak English. And I'm so exhausted after seven years on the road that I can barely travel a mile into town on a good day to hoist a margarita straight up in memory of the athlete I once was.

While we had our final hockey-playing seasons in the sun, though, Em and I flaunted them, believe me. And of all the articles about my athletic exploits that I ever clipped from a newspaper in my long and mediocre career, the favorite one by far is this, torn from the Albuquerque *Journal* on Wednesday, February 9, 1972:

FALCONS WIN, 14 — 10

Em Hall and John Nichols each scored seven goals — yep, seven goals each — as the Falcons swooped on the Rockets, 14–10, in New Mexico Hockey League action.

Jim Manguso and Scott Allman each scored three goals for the losers. For the Rockets, Vic Ramponi had a busy night as the Falcons slapped 59 shots his way.

Falcons	6 2	6 — 14
Rockets	2 5	3 — 10

F — Em Hall 7 goals and 6 assists; John Nichols 7 goals and 4 assists.

R — Jim Manguso 3 goals and 2 assists; Scott Allman 3 goals and one assist.

Early morning, upper Taos Valley

Moon setting over Tres Orejas

Occasionally, these days, Em gives me a call on the phone. "Oye, Gabacho," he croaks in his gravelly, cigaretted-out voice: "I'm coming to Taos, Pendejo. Let's tomar a lonche together, si tienes un chansey, O.K.? Mi troca no tiene brekes, but I think I can make it. Orale, primo-cuate: take it suave. Ay te watcho, caramacho. Goodbye."

You may not understand what he's saying, but I guarantee, there's more chutzpah and life in that convoluted Spanglish slang than ever came out of Brooklyn!

In February, the 1970 winter suddenly ended. Snow melted, and everyone who had cursed January's freezing weather worried about February's drought. Dire predictions about a dry summertime circled the valley. Down in the front field, using a weed cutter, I chopped brown grass. All around Ranchitos farmers who had not grazed their land after last autumn's final cutting, burned the short dead grass: a pungent smoke hung over the valley. Warm days had the Taos Ski Valley writhing from lack of snow. Smelling springtime in the air, I assumed winter was more or less over. While I swung the weed cutter, our two cats prowled the exposed areas, hunting mice. Wrapped in a comforter on our side lawn, Ruby boned up on Cuba while four horses from Phil Lavadie's field stood patiently at the fence waiting for handouts of carrots or rotten crab apples.

I raked the dry grass into big piles, and Luke helped me pitch it into the VW bus. We dumped it between the basketball hoop and the western fence around the chicken coop. At dusk, three black Angus bulls in Lavadie's field put their heads together, and, grunting amicably, they pushed each other around, lazily — almost gently — fighting. Lying down side by side in the field, Luke and I stared up at the white half-moon, and smelled the burnt fields of Ranchitos. A cat settled on my stomach and kneaded my flesh, purring quietly. The horse in Tom Trujillo's pasture snorted impatiently, asking us to pitch over another forkful of hay. Then in the bright darkness, whinnying from spring juices rising, the horses in fields on both sides of us thundered around at a gallop, squealing and rear-

ing up against the fences, racing off and then thundering toward us again.

Lavadie's fence is located only five feet from our bedroom wall, and occasionally it would seem as if those oversexed, galloping monsters might crash right through the wall while we were making love, or just lying there quietly, or sound asleep and dreaming.

I drove Ruby and a friend to Austin, where they caught a plane for Mexico City and Cuba. While Ruby was down there, Luke and I led a quiet life. We played tackle football in the front field; we raked up all the yard leaves and set them on fire. I walked around playing old Pink Anderson and Reverend Gary Davis tunes on my guitar while the leaves crackled, and Luke lounged in our new hay pile, fascinated by the flames.

I felt paranoid because a congressional committee headed by Senator Eastland was trying to subpoena the records of Liberation News Service in New York, to whom I had contributed some money a few years ago. If they did, I figured I would come under the uncomfortable scrutiny of the FBI or another police organization. Too, after five years of political awareness, demonstrations, culture shock, I was tired, sick to death of the U.S.A. I wondered what it would be like to emigrate to Canada, getting off the hook. I was tired of awaking each morning with the deeds of American imperialism and American history and bigotry weighing heavy on my mind. To hell with that responsibility! How could I forge a break? Why couldn't I simply float through life in an appreciative, self-indulgent way, wearing colorful clothes and singing songs, bearing no responsibility for the sins of my forefathers, for the sins of my nation's army, for the misery of places like Vietnam, or ghettos in Detroit and Washington, D.C.? If I had to live in rural, rustic Taos, why not enjoy the life instead of always keeping in mind the brutal poverty around me, the oppression, the bitter struggle it was for my neighbors to hang on to their tiny farms, shreds of dignity, their dreams.

Being torn between political activism and novel writing created in me a powerful fatigue. Perhaps the two were incompatible. How could a novel launched by a straight publisher have an "effect" on things. Better to write pure propaganda, and man the barricades.

Impossible, it seemed, to focus, find a correct rhythm. How to correlate what instinctively I *wanted* to do in life with what I felt — morally, ethically — I *should* do in life? The old bourgeois emotional roots ran deep; and my position of privilege was hard to jeopardize totally by becoming a truly honest radical.

After an explosion in a New York town house that killed three unidentified Weatherpeople, the radio claimed members of Weathermen were in Cuba learning to build bombs under the guise of cutting sugarcane. Sensing a new McCarthy era warming up, I felt terribly dejected. In my journal I wrote: "I grow incredibly weary with the specter of goon squads wiping out whatever gentle and humanistic and sincerely caring people remain in this country." While I was in town, distributing moratorium leaflets, a man followed behind me, yanking the leaflets off automobile windshields and ripping them in half. Politely, I asked him to quit it. He told me, "I hate people who don't support the draft." I shrugged, and continued leafleting; he kept following, destroying my leaflets. Finally, he shouted, "If you don't like this country why don't you fucking leave it?" I couldn't believe he had actually used that cliché.

An uneasy time pulled at the Taos Valley. The "hippie problem," dormant since late last summer, began to occupy everyone's mind. Rumors said over twenty-five thousand freaks would pass through town in the summer of 1970. By mid-March, already, so many transient newcomers had entered the area that the situation had reached a premature crisis point. Letters to the editor of the Taos *News* had become shrill, almost hysterical. A war was brewing; the smell of blood was in the air. Liberals and conservatives had squared off in mortal combat long before the first shots were fired. I thought of it as theater, manipulated consciously or unconsciously by forces and people who stood to gain much from the chaos that would result.

In the second week of March, snow fell. Hundreds of meadowlarks, redwing blackbirds, and robins descended from the sky along with the white stuff. Perched on fence posts, they sang vibrantly while the storm settled on the land.

The snow was gone immediately, however; and then it was time to clean the acequias, an ongoing spring ritual, now, for hundreds of years. In general, though it fluctuates slightly according to the customs of each ditch, every landowner must supply one man to work one day for every five acres he or she owns. Although I own only 1.7 acres, my front and back fields are irrigated by two different ditches, so I commenced my knowledge of how acequias, and their politics, function by laboring with two different crews on separate weekends, breaking my back (and destroying my citified hands) in the process.

The Taos area is green thanks entirely to the intricate network of major irrigation ditches and laterals carrying water to every nook and cranny of the valley in exactly the same way that the human arterial system carries blood throughout our bodies. In every community a number of separate (though similarly organized) ditches transport crucial river water to the land. Three commissioners and a mayordomo (the ditch boss), elected by people whose land is watered by the acequia, govern each ditch and its laterals. The commissioners oversee financial, legal, and political problems connected with the ditch: the mayordomo deals directly with physical maintenance and apportionment of water during the irrigation season. If a landowner won't work on the ditch, or hire workers to take his place, he will not receive water for his fields during the spring and summer months.

For centuries, in an area where commerce has been based almost entirely on agriculture, land without water rights has been next to useless. Hence the acequia system and its attendant politics have been at the structural heart of all aspects of life. Today, as more and more land is removed from farm production because of urban expansion, housing developments, and the destruction of an agrarian-based culture, the irrigation systems are breaking down. Many newcomers have little knowledge of the importance acequia politics hold in keeping land, community, and culture together: they ignore their water rights, build houses in the middle of former alfalfa fields, and have little interest in learning about or supporting the old-fashioned lifeblood structures. Developers constantly buy up the water rights of destitute old-timers, transferring them to municipal or commercial endeavors. Other long-time users, tired of fighting against the overwhelming odds presented by this changing society, and demoralized by the collapse of venerated structures and families, lose interest: instead of working on the acequias themselves, or paying men decent wages to perform the hard work necessary to keep the ditches in good shape, they hire boys cheap, and the kids do a half-baked job. In due course, an ancient organization which lies at the heart of communal control of the valley's destiny is corrupted, and begins to die. As it collapses, people lose touch with each other, families become more private and alienated, the subsistence infrastructure unravels, and communities flounder, their political power lost as a different system takes over.

I did not think about all this back then: I merely learned that I was supposed to clean two acequias, so I went and cleaned two acequias. And I loved the work. I was accompanied by perhaps thirty men and boys, all speaking Spanish, who joked a lot, castigating each other, and ran down local politics, rumors, scandals, heartaches. In a line we entered the ditch, chain-gang style, and chopped at the banks, dug out mud and brush and rocks from the bottom, built up the sides, and cursed our lot. We dropped wooden matches into thick brown grasses lining the banks and leaned on our shovels while the grasses burned, casting a thick blue smoke across the flat beige fields where horses and sheep stood still, waiting for the smog to dissipate. Sometimes we dug up still hibernating frogs from the mud: they quivered, trying to stretch, puzzled by this sudden unearthing. Men casually stabbed apart little water snakes with their shovel blades. And killdeers raced around us, screeching loudly.

It was hard work, but it felt good: and I learned a lot, listening to the talk. I learned who owned each piece of land, and about the hated patrons of the village, as well as the respected old geezers. I heard stories of land scams and feuds. I was the butt of some friendly, but heavily loaded, anti-gringo teasing. In the end, we had cleaned, dug out, and reinforced a ditch for yet another year in exactly the same manner as that ditch had been cleaned since its construction one or maybe two hundred years ago. Exhausted, I staggered home to sit on my portal staring at the mountains while demolishing a six-pack of beer. Magpies taunted me from nearby cottonwoods.

A month later, I cut water into my little back field for the first time. I'd enjoy saying that I handled this, and subsequent irrigations, like a seasoned trooper, sending tons of water exactly where I wanted them to go simply by plopping a single shovelful of mud (as I have seen hundreds of old-timers do) into the proper place at the proper time, and then resting on my shovel handle in the warm apple-blossom-scented day while the physical laws of water flow completed the job.

Unfortunately, I manhandled my first watering (and many subsequent irrigations) more as Jerry Lewis, Laurel and Hardy, or Charlie Chaplin might have done it. Throwing open a small wooden head gate, I set the acequia's ample contents roaring into my field ... whereupon approximately a ton of water a minute disappeared — like a draining bathtub — into a single gopher hole barely four inches wide! Frantically, I dug up shovelfuls of earth, filling in the hole. But my field is not level; and three minutes later I had a muddy torrent zipping down its center, churning through my just planted garden and carrying away all the seeds, then inundating my driveway, practically tumbling the VW bus into my front field! Racing about frantically, I slammed down the head gate, only to discover that I hadn't built up the ditch bank high enough: gushes of water overflowed every ten feet. Staggering back and forth, I shoveled up reams of mud, trying to build little dams here, forge small channels there. Like a human backhoe stuck in some frenetic excavating gear, I charged around my tiny field, shifting preposterous mountains of heavy muck in order to dampen that little plot of ground. In the end, a job which should have taken a half hour cost me the entire day. To be truthful, I actually labored well into the night!

That wasn't the last time, either, that I have wound up out there, stomping about in my leaky irrigation boots, trying to guide water by a flashlight held against the handle of my frenetically chopping shovel. Because I am an Anglo, and because my land is at the end of a long lateral, I am often allocated water from sundown to sunup, a time period that makes for some interesting problems. Come dark, I walk a mile along Upper Ranchitos Road, and cut in my water off the main Lovatos ditch. Then I must travel every inch of the ditch in the dark, making sure everyone's head gates along the way are shut tightly so that none of my water will be diverted before it reaches my field. I do this in terror, barked at by dozens of vicious dogs, and wondering when some trigger-happy neighbor, thinking that I am a robber or a rapist, will cut loose on me with a .270 rifle or a 12-gauge shotgun. Finally, the water reaches my field, and I stumble around with my weak-beamed flashlight (cursing myself for forgetting to buy batteries!) trying to see how the water is flowing. Inevitably, the muddy lifeblood suddenly stops entering my brome and alfalfa, and I must reconnoiter the ditch to find out who opened a head

Trout country, the Pueblo River gorge

gate, either illegally or through having failed to check with the mayordomo to see if the water was already allocated elsewhere.

Occasionally, when my water flow has abruptly stopped at midnight, I've given up and, exhausted, neglecting to close off my head gates, I've gone to bed, only to awaken at dawn to discover that somebody cut the water back in while I slept, and my house and entire lands are flooded, the garden ruined, the fruit trees drowned, turds from the overflowing septic tank floating against my portal, and the chickens swimming like ducks around their inundated pen!

I guess it has been anguishing sometimes. Yet I could recount abundant other moments when irrigating has been a truly soul-reinforcing activity. For many's the peaceful mist-ridden morning or late bright summer afternoon that I've stood by my back ditch, or on the banks of the front-field acequia, lazily watching the water trickle into my green grass while grackles, blackbirds, and magpies gather to eat the bugs and worms driven to the surface, and I've thought that this job of applying water to my fields is one of my best shots for making it into the twenty-first century.

On March 18 a good friend called from New York City to say that a woman killed in that town-house "bomb factory" blast a couple of weeks earlier had just been identified as Diana Oughton. He had known her well and loved her deeply, and, although I had not been with her often, through him I felt an important intimacy with the woman, and with her life and her political struggle. The two men closest to me had known Diana well and considered her one of this country's more special human beings. Through my friends' feelings for her she had become an important person to me, a personal symbol to hold in my heart of the struggle of our times.

"Are you all right?" I asked, stunned. And repeated it inanely: "Are you all right?"

"Sure. I don't want to talk about it, though. Not on the phone . . ."

"Will you write me a letter?"

"I'll write you a letter."

I said I didn't know what to say. He said there was nothing to say. "It happened."

"I love you," I blurted into the phone. "I'm sorry. I love you —"

We hung up, and I walked into the back field and stood there feeling sick and numb and frightened and really angry at all the violence. Benevolent snowstorms swept scarf-like through the gray mountains. A flock of bluebirds surrounded me, landing on the heads of sunflowers and flapping their wings rapidly, trying to stay upright as the plants bent over from their weight. Earlier that day I had talked with a hippie neighbor, in the National Guard, who had been ordered to cut his hair. He had refused, and asked me whether or not I thought it was worth going through a court-martial for refusing to obey that order. About Diana I couldn't determine what to think or feel. Who to blame, what to blame? I felt very queasy. Senator Eastland was grabbing headlines by claiming that all these crazy lefties were learning bomb-making skills on Venceremos Brigades in Cuba. Numerous friends back in New York were working with different organizations — I had already forgotten some of their names; out West I had lost touch. Committees, organizing, caucuses — the radical left, many aspects, all aspects. The Communist Party was there somewhere, so were others: RU, OL, budding revolutionaries who called the CPUSA revisionist and dominated by the CIA. The infighting was confusing, depressing. There were Maoists, Trotskyists, Spartacists — this, that, and the other thing.

The weather against Taos Mountain melted into the forests, leaving an indeterminate afterglow.

I stood in my back field trying to deal with the death of a woman who had loved, and been loved by, my close friend. I did not agree with her means, but I believed that her understanding of, and instincts about, our society, the world economic situation, and history were correct. Her idealism was powerful and important. And, no matter what anybody will ever say, I know she was a fiercely compassionate and immensely loving person. Already I cringed, projecting myself forward into newspaper headlines calling her a perverted, sexually deviant, psychologically disturbed terrorist. I was twenty-nine years old, and Diana was around the same age.

We had been members of the Silent Generation in college. And already our generation was dying.

I retrieved some back newspapers stored in the garage and, squatting in the dirt driveway, reread articles about the explosion that had demolished a Greenwich Village town house, in which three bodies had been found, unrecognizable, two men, one woman.

Next day the papers published her picture, taken from a police photograph at a lineup after the Chicago Days of Rage. It didn't look anything like her. It looked tough, hard as nails, roughed-up, mean, ugly, fanatical. What could the supposedly light-sensitive film in that policeman's camera have been thinking?

I stood in the back field again, facing the mountain. A sense of loss and uncertainty had me feeling very strange. I had met Diana eight years earlier, in Guatemala, a colonial country then in one of its perennial states of siege, a beautiful, miserably impoverished nation that will stay that way so long as the United States chooses to support the exploitation of its people. Diana had been sent to Guatemala by the American Friends: the despair of the Quiche Maya among whom she worked had nourished her radical roots.

Tourists travel to, and businesses locate in, Guatemala for the same reason they are likely to travel to, or locate in, Taos County. The landscape is beautiful; the cultures and history are diverse, and both spiritually and academically nourishing; and people have been kept down for so long that they can be had for a song.

The simple tenet that applies here is that it is not right for people to live that way.

Taos Mountain, in Taos County, New Mexico, U.S.A., overlooks a beautiful Pueblo where the per capita cash income for a family of four is less than a thousand dollars a year, alcoholism is a serious problem, and too many residents have too little hope for the future.

But their Pueblo is very photogenic, and the tourists flock there in droves.

I remembered the last time I had seen Diana, in my friend's apartment. I had arrived there while he was out getting a paper. Wearing his pajamas, she was sitting up on a couch, and had a cold. I said, "Hi," and we chatted a little until my friend returned; we talked about this, that, nothing important. On the wall behind her was a poster, a picture of Ché Guevara, and, at the base of the poster, a quotation from one of his speeches: "At the risk of seeming ridiculous, let me say that the true revolutionary is guided by great feelings of love."

Diana looked a bit pixieish in those big pajamas. A sore throat had reduced her voice to a whisper: her mouth looked lush, her face was soft, flushed. I thought of . . . was it Paulette Goddard I had once seen in a film, looking beautiful in Charlie Chaplin's too big pajamas?

That was my final image of Diana.

Later, my friend wrote a letter. In it he said many things that were related in one way or another to the event, to her life and to the lives of us all in those times, to what were the right and correct and important things to be working toward. He made no judgments about her methods, although I had always understood he disagreed with what could only be a suicidal violence. Somewhere in the letter, finally, he said that they had made love only the night before Diana left, and disappeared, and then died. And he was grateful for that. Because if you had to say goodbye to someone, that was the best way to say goodbye: making love.

I stood out in the back field after hearing about Diana, and knew that there is no escaping historical obligations, and that the beauty of mountains means nothing if there is no passionate commitment to the human society dwelling in their shadows.

It was time to go out, do more, learn things, discover people, take a tougher stand.

Late winter, Taos Mountain

Part V

STRUGGLES

There is a profound and pervasive difference in the way Anglos and Spanish-Americans relate to land.... Spanish-Americans tend to have an emotional attachment to the land (it is part of the family) and to value intimate, personal knowledge of one's own land and a continued lineal-family land ownership. They emphasize land transfer-and-use decisions based upon community welfare, along with the view that land ownership and usage established by custom are more important than those based upon legal documents. Anglos tend to view land as a commodity to be bought and sold if the price is right, and to stress maximum monetary income from land while they hold it.

— CLYDE EASTMAN, GARREY CARRUTHERS, and JAMES A. LIEFER, "Contrasting Attitudes Toward Land in New Mexico"

Taos County may be beautiful, but it is not a happy environment for many of its nineteen-thousand inhabitants. Only yesterday — May 6, 1977 — the local social services director told me approximately 43 percent of the county is on one form of welfare or another. Although many long-time local people (including those on welfare) tend to own their own houses, having kept them in the family, through inheritance, for centuries, much of that housing is now substandard:

the subsistence infrastructure of mutual aid has broken down, and poor people have no cash for repairs. Within city limits outhouses are still common: over half the dwellings in the county lack adequate plumbing; a quarter of the houses are overcrowded. Outhouses, inadequate drainage in low-lying areas, poorly constructed septic tanks, and hand-dug wells mean that much of the water supply is polluted, leading to endemic low-profile diseases such as constant colds, which are a real drain on the poor. In town, there is very little low- or middle-income housing, especially for the elderly. And the wealthy in-migrants of recent years have driven real estate prices so high almost nobody local can afford to buy land or build decent houses.

Because at least half the population is extremely poor, the county has a weak tax base and cannot provide adequate services to meet growth needs. Already a new sewage plant, built to replace the old one which had been condemned by the EIA, is badly oversubscribed.

County unemployment is high. Official figures, almost always misleading, fail to include people not actively seeking employment. The work situation is so hopeless many jobless gave up long ago. Others pridefully reject the poverty occupations available here, choosing instead to eke out a living on their remaining tiny land parcels. Hence, although the official unemployment rate for Taos, according to Employment Security Commission statistics of two years ago, fluctuated from a high of 17.7 percent in February to a low of 10.4 in September, the actual rate is much higher. Immediately to the east and west, in largely Spanish-speaking Rio Arriba and Mora counties, the *official* unemployment rates for the same period were staggering: a high of 37.4 percent in Mora, 25.4 percent in Rio Arriba.

Most of the jobs available in this land of tourism and little else are service-oriented, low-paying, seasonal. They perpetuate poverty instead of alleviating it. Marginal families are hurt badly by the uncertain and erratic labor market. They buy on time while employed at the height of the season in July, and suffer repossessions when laid off in October. If they mortgage a possession when cash is coming in, they can lose a car, a piece of land, even a home when the off-season layoffs occur. Hence, a desperate marginal hustle harries most of the local scufflers. Too, approximately ten thousand people in the Taos—Rio Arriba area work as migrant farmers in surrounding states during the growing season or for sheep outfits up North. U.S. Civil Rights Commission reports have said that many of these people are sometimes forced to work under conditions "resembling involuntary servitude or peonage." Some Taoseños follow the lambing seasons, starting in February down South and heading North to Wyoming and Montana, where the lambing occurs in late spring. All these jobs are traditionally low-paying; the cash earned is barely enough to meet the costs of hanging on to property in Taos County. Absence from the county also tends to weaken households and communities, making them that much more vulnerable to the outside exploitation gearing to take over the county, making it a recreation and retirement paradise.

Within Taos proper, given the amount of work involved and the patronizing abuse that must be suffered, there is often a better shot at dignity by asking for welfare instead of applying for the dishwashing, cook, waitressing, chambermaid type of jobs. More lucrative employment traditionally reserved for locals — as seamstresses or cutters in local moccasin or dress factories — barely pays minimum wage. Still, earnings of $3,000 to $4,000 a year are almost decent pay in the county. Union activity, outside of food chain stores and the Questa molybdenum mine, is almost nil. Agitators are quickly fired; any

number of people desperate for cash can be found to take their places.

In a recent survey I made, I found that of 132 businesses located at the heart of Taos, on or immediately around the Plaza, 107 (or approximately 80 percent) were owned by Anglos. In a town apocryphally rumored to be the world's third-largest art center (after Paris and New York) in terms of volume of paintings sold, 32 out of 36 galleries listed in the local phone directory are Anglo-owned. Out of 23 listed real estate businesses, 21 are Anglo operations, as are two out of three major auto dealerships. 40 out of 52 listed restaurants are owned by more recent arrivals to the area, as are 10 out of the 12 listed sporting-goods operations. 54 out of 57 listed motels and hotels are Anglo-owned. Ditto with both the local AM and FM radio stations. Listed Anglo contractors outnumber local contractors 15—3. Among professionals such as lawyers, doctors, and dentists, the breakdown is equally lopsided: Anglo lawyers outnumbering Chicano lawyers 19—4, Anglos outnumber local doctors 19—2, and local dentists 7—1.

There is no question that long-time local Taoseños control the electoral politics: but the real economic power that guides society resides in relative newcomers' hands.

Over the last ten years, an influx of newcomers has enormously altered the area. Escapees from urban blight, often independently wealthy or folks who made a bundle in New York or Los Angeles, or people like myself who can earn a living outside the county, they have turned Taos upside down: and, often unintentionally, they are forging the type of nightmare they fled only a few years earlier, creating an unstable and selfish environment that will become as crowded and uninhabitable and frenzied as much of the rest of the nation.

The little five-room house and 1.7 acres I bought for $14,500 in 1969 could probably go today, to an in-migrating middle-class person, for from $50,000 to $60,000. That's with the horrendous plumbing, wood heat in the kitchen and bedrooms, non-functioning septic tank, the dirt roof, and the insanely potholed driveway — the whole rustic, aggravating schmeer. Land where I live cost about $1,000 an acre when I arrived: now it's easily $8,000 an acre. My next-door neighbor is asking $18,000 for a two-acre parcel, and sooner rather than later he'll probably get it. This kind of pricing knocks most Chicanos right out of the market. In fact, when a neighbor's nephew, who badly wants to stay in Taos County, asked his uncle to sell him some land, the uncle replied flatly, "You couldn't afford it." Everybody is selling to newcomers these days. And, because the private land with water rights is so limited, the metaphor applying to the in- and out-migration pattern occurring here is that of a completely full cup of water from which, every time a drop falls in, another drop spills out.

The dogfight occurring over limited, unexpandable resources here is not pleasant to watch. Most of the available land now belongs to, or is being developed by, outsiders. I mentioned earlier that the Forest Service controls 45 percent of the county. Five years ago, in an article for the *New Mexico Review*, I broke down the pattern of ownership for much of the remaining land — a pattern that still holds true today — in the following fashion:

A large portion — over 10,000 acres — of the Gijosa Grant is owned by a strange and confusing conglomerate of the Klauer Corporation and the B-Bar-H Corporation out of Colorado, which form the Ranchos Land and Orchard Company, one part of which is the Vista Linda Subdivision whose lots are owned almost entirely by out-of-state residents. Next door, Melvin Weimer, a Colorado Springs businessman, owns approximately 8,000 acres of the La Serna Grant. Red River is owned almost entirely by out-of-state people: J. P. Brandenburg's First State Bank there is operated seasonally, open only from June 1 through September 15. Taos Canyon is almost entirely under vacation-type development, seasonal homes owned exclusively by out-of-staters. The area west of the Rio Grande not within Carson National Forest, Public Domain, BLM, or state-owned lands, seems at a cursory glance to belong to either Patrick Kirby's Kirby Cattle Company (he's from Pasadena, California), or to a number of huge subdivisions bought into by easterners and midwesterners, such as the Tres Piedras Estates' 5,760 acres, Taos Estates, Highland Estates, Carson Estates, and so forth —

And much of this largely sagebrush land was recently purchased by Japanese corporations at a tax auction.

The rest of the Taos Valley is being changed from a stable, agrarian, Spanish-speaking area of strong individual communities held together by cultural ties, into a retirement-recreation, middle-class suburban, ghettoized urban mess, and the change is occurring with stunning rapidity. Little planning, lackluster zoning, and no overall philosophy are guiding it. The progress motto seems to be "every man for himself, and the devil take the hindmost."

Three Saturdays ago I was cleaning the Pacheco ditch beside an old man who told me: "I think we are almost at the end of this acequia farming. I think the ditch systems will collapse; I think it's almost over. All the local people are so discouraged. You can't earn a living off the land any more, or find fields to rent for your cattle."

Few of the newcomers here bother to learn Spanish, or to become involved in the crucial land and water politics. Their interests are more self-oriented than communal, and so the communal sense is dying. Newcomers will organize to try and stop a few pretty trees from being cut down by highway crews, but will rarely attend meetings about a proposed powerful taxing district that could efficiently wipe out the remaining rural population. Being middle-class in a nation whose middle-class population tends to move every couple of years, they come in for short stays, then leave, creating an unhealthy transient ethic in the county, which further undermines community roots.

Thanks to the in-migration, competition for jobs — even marginal jobs — has become brutal. Many college-bred Anglos have invaded the turf of service employment and knocked off even those jobs. Hippies, often comfortably in control of trust funds or other parental financial safety valves, are taking over even the waitress, cook, and bottle-washer jobs. Ph.D.s, out to groove on a simpler life, earn a bundle in New York or San Francisco, move to Taos, buy up land at egregiously inflated prices, build their own houses, and then become carpenters, who are of course hired by others of their own ilk moving into the area. Hence formerly middle-class Anglos threaten to dominate such trades as plumbing and carpentry; they are increasingly being hired for the construction jobs generated by English-speaking, middle-class recent arrivals. Right now there is a housing boom in Taos, as the county twitches and groans on its way toward middle-classhood. But most of the permanent adobe construction is being financed by newcomers and contracted by newcomers who can afford the prices.

Imprint of magpie wings in snow

Talpa hills, five miles southeast of Taos

Local folks, their children desperate to hang on to a bit of their land and heritage, are reduced to living in trailers and cheap frame houses.

In 1950, Taos County was 81 percent Spanish-speaking. By 1960 it was 69 percent Spanish-speaking. Today, this trend continues.

Most of the long-time people in the tightly knit northern communities were involved in subsistence or small-time cash agriculture. Today, farming as a way of life here is going the way of the dinosaur, with no viable alternative mode of survival to replace it. Between 1954 and 1964, the total number of farms in Taos County decreased 43.8 percent. According to a 1972 Economic Base Analysis of the county by city planner José Yguado, out of 610 farms in the county, 531 grossed less than $2,500. 214 of those farms earned between $250 and $1,000. 220 others earned under $250. "For the northern New Mexico area," wrote Mr. Yguado, "it is estimated that a commercial farm has to make $10,000 in order to profit."

A local saying claims that a man with one acre and a cow is a rancher. True enough, but not exactly funny. Until recently, a family owning only a few acres of land on which they gardened could supplement home-grown foods and orchard produce by running sheep and cattle on communal land or on permits in the National Forest. For decades, however, the National Forest has been managed as a business enterprise with little sympathy for local ranchers, and today the permit situation has reached crisis proportions.

Recently, a friend who works for the Forest Service (Floresta) asked me to have a drink with him. In the Taos Inn he presented me with a copy of the Floresta's recent review of their Multiple Use planning and management philosophy. Flipping through the paper to a section dealing with government attitudes toward local residents of the Carson Forest area, he asked me to read it. The statement said the government must make serious attempts to include local people in its planning. It must have respect for their cultural heritage and ranching practices, and bend over backwards to include the Spanish-speaking and Native American people in the evolution of its forestry philosophy and practices.

When I had finished, my friend said, "John, I really have trouble with this section of our guidelines. I mean, it's nice rhetoric, but it doesn't mean squat. There's hardly anything the government does, or intends to do in the future, which seems compatible with these highfalutin' statements."

What he meant was this: The Carson Forest — nearly half of Taos County — is managed primarily for timbering, mining, and recreation interests. For that reason it is becoming ever more difficult for marginal ranchers to maintain their hold on National Forest permits. For years, if one farmer sold out to another, the number of animals allowed on his permit was reduced by 10 percent. A government requirement that cattle owners fence animals out of the National Forest has resulted in heavy expenditure by small ranchers for fencing. When cattle stray onto federal land, or overstep their unfenced forest permit areas, a severe impoundment and fine system further oppresses the small farmer. For years, grazing fees on Forest Service and Bureau of Land Management terrain have been raised two cents per animal unit each year, adding further economic pressure against the small operator. Currently, the fees stand at $1.51 a.u.m. (animal unit per month) for cattle, and $0.30 a.u.m. for sheep. A recent proposal to jack up the cattle fees to $1.89 a.u.m. has met with stern opposition, and whether the fees will eventually achieve that level is up to the United States Congress.

While the Forest Service complains that sheep cause severe environmental damage by overgrazing land, it builds rest areas along the wild river section of the Rio Grande, thereby sucking in tourists and adding immeasurably to the environmental destruction of that area. Too, though the Forest Service is willing to construct dozens of garish picnic cubicles beside the Rio Grande just north of Pilar, they can't seem to build a stock tank or drill a well in Pacomio Mondragón's lambing area west of the Rio Grande near Carson. Meaning that Pacomio must spend almost three hours daily hauling water from the river in a tank truck.

The prejudice is not subtle. And for that reason Smokey the Bear has become a disliked and distrusted symbol in the North. For just as it became official government policy to destroy the buffalo in order to subdue the Plains Indians, and just as the Bureau of Indian Affairs has long been a bureau of oppression rather than of protection of Native American rights, the Floresta in northern New Mexico has been in constant conflict with the aspirations and life styles of the indigenous inhabitants.

Since I arrived in Taos, there have been many struggles for land and water, for the right to exist in traditional ways, also for the privilege to exploit natural resources and the human community. Some of these struggles, such as Reies Tijerina's land-grant movement, have involved thousands of people; others have been small, involving only an individual, or the several dozen irrigators on a lone acequia.

I started learning about these struggles in March of 1970, shortly after Diana Oughton died. A friend took me up to Questa to meet his cousin, who had just been fired by the molybdenum mine on an apparently trumped-up charge. I met José Cisneros and his wife, Mary Ann, on a soft, overcast day, with intermittent snowflakes falling. And as I listened to their stories, a process began which would change the way I lived my life in Taos over the next few years.

The situation was traditional, banal — oft repeated in this country, taken for granted. José had challenged the corporate power and a sweetheart union by relentlessly filing grievance reports over what he felt were unfair working conditions. He had filed discrimination complaints with the U. S. Department of Labor over the lack of Raza foremen at the mine. And he had filed charges in retaliation to actions taken against him by the mine. In return, he felt that he had been fired for making waves. Enraged, José had decided to fight back. He was talking to the NLRB, the EEOC, the Mexican-American Legal Defense Fund. He wanted me to write an article for a magazine or a newspaper, publicizing his case.

During the afternoon we discussed union politics; also the way an aunt's land was being taken in a quiet title suit. José paused to deliver a dissertation on how he'd made an air compressor from an old refrigerator motor and a discarded electric sander. In fact, we covered everything from cultural genocide to the lambing just starting in the valley, to the process by which the moly mine's entrance into Questa had driven up taxes, causing some locals who had no mine jobs to actually lose their land thanks to the valley's industrial good fortune.

When I left, I wrote a long article about José's fight, and sent it to the New Mexico Review, a muckraking liberal magazine published monthly in Santa Fe, and distributed rather erratically around the state.

From the moment they published the article, I had a forum, a reason for actively learning more about the North, for focusing my feelings and my understanding of the area.

Almost everything anyone did for that magazine was voluntary. The original publisher, Ed Schwartz, once gave me a fifty-dollar check, but it was the only bread I saw in two years of writing a long investigative article almost every month. Still, the Review gave me a reason for being. It literally saved my life as the frustrating years between novels stretched to five, then six, then seven. And I met and worked with people who loved and cherished New Mexico: they had a right-on politics and wanted to fight the destruction of this fragile land and the people who have guarded it for generations. Contributors were as well known as Stan Steiner and the Albuquerque environmentalists Katherine and Peter Montague; they were as dedicated as Joan Friedland, a lawyer for the Santa Fe Community Law Center, who for years was one of the few sympathetic mouthpieces for oppressed and radical people in the North. Given the "gift" of the floundering Review when Ed Schwartz departed the scene, Em Hall and Jim Bensfield nursed it along on a wing and a Hail Mary as a quasi-collective, dreaming of making it a southwestern New Yorker, even as half their contributing editors struggled to fashion it into the leftist propaganda arm of New Mexico's transplanted-from-New York radic-lib community. At the same time, the magazine's financial sources urged the Review to become a kind of Barry Commoner scholastic magazine and ecological lobbying blat supporting the state's conservation forces.

Over the next two and a half years, I wrote many articles on the North. The writing helped me learn about the land, people, and history of the area; and about the situation existing today. I had the luck to meet some of the most together men and women I have ever run across in my life. Occasionally, I also found myself engaging in uncomfortable tête-à-têtes with bona fide scoundrels.

New Mexico is a state with barely a million population; hence it is like a small town, and it's very difficult to hide here. Several times, in public meetings, I have been accused of being an outside agitator. A lawyer, who was subsequently busted and incarcerated in the state penitentiary for embezzling from his own firm, once threatened to sue me for using the word "shenanigans" to describe his court tactics during a tense conservancy district hearing. Another lawyer, about to retire from that same case shortly after a *Review* article badgered him about his obvious conflict of interest, called me up at seven one morning, said, "You speak Spanish, don't you, John?" and proceeded to curse me out in that language, lathering me in a string of peppy obscenities while I groggily muttered, "Huh? . . . What? . . . Come again?" Over the telephone even little old ladies have ordered me to keep my nose clean and out of other folks' dirty linen. Once, when I was doing background research on an undercover agent who had triggered a double-slaying stakeout in which a radical friend of mine was murdered while allegedly stealing dynamite, the agent appeared in Taos to get information on my work from people who had talked with me, and I spent an ugly paranoid time worrying about my life. No bullets have hit my house or my car, however, although one evening, while I lay in the haymow gazing up at cottonwoods shedding their fluffy spring snow, a rifle blasted down by the river a hundred yards away, and a slug tore through the cottonwood branches high above my head, giving me pause for more than a moment.

Mostly, however, the articles opened my life onto a time and a place. And the people I met through the articles conferred upon me their sense of what it means to have a historical continuity in every day, in every mood of weather, in every piece of news about a neighbor, in every characteristic of landscape.

The other day, Bill Davis was talking to me about an old man, José María Mondragón, whose son, Pacomio, is among the last of the valley's sheepmen. Their farm stands just behind my friend Justin Locke's old house on the Llano Quemado ridge. The father is a tiny stooped man who walks with a cane. Bill described to me how he once saw the old man slowly toil up a nearby foothill, turn, and plant his cane firmly, overlooking the Ranchos-Talpa Valley. "But he wasn't just seeing it as we know it today," Bill said. "He could see it from its inception in his eyes as a child. He saw superimposed over the present scene a thousand different layers of landscape and weather, development and history—"

I could imagine his complex vision: of houses that have crumbled, and land—once pasture—that has gone unirrigated for decades, returning to sagebrush; and of all the people who owned farms and lost them, intermarried, moved away. An entire history superimposed on the serene valley—famous floods, famous blizzards, famous murders, old sweethearts, long-gone flocks of sheep, the dirt path that became a highway and the first cars that traveled the new artery. Layer upon historical layer. And I thought: How strong and complex that image must be. How profoundly centered is a person who can stand like that at the heart of his community, its life and history, feeling it all familiar and real, however prolific the ghosts that have evaporated for all time—

Owning this valley in his heart.

Such a gift of historical and cultural continuity my own family gave to me with the Mastic house, and William Floyd, and all the journals and stories that have accumulated through the centuries reaffirming our sense of ourselves, keeping strong the connection between generations, making certain the sensation of being a North American is something much more than the disoriented rootlessness plaguing so many of us today. And that background made it important to accept from the people of this valley the gift of their own historical continuity, embracing this landscape not because it is picture-postcard beautiful, but because of the human legends and histories and personalities that transform the natural world into a living part of the complex social organism.

The year 1970 in particular was hectic, paranoid, and often violent in Taos County. It began with the so-called hippie-Chicano war and drew to a close with some bombings of Forest Service installations attributed to the Taos Pueblo's struggle for the return of its sacred Blue Lake land. The year concluded with a major triumph when the United States Senate voted 70–12 in favor of the Taos Indians' Blue Lake bill. Despite that landmark victory, the people of Taos County were divided, conquered, broken up into factions; their outrage over years of exploitation had been expertly defused during a time of political and intellectual ferment that could have resulted in powerful and lasting social changes guaranteeing to long-time local residents their land and water rights for a much longer time than it now appears those amenities are slated to last.

December, Rio Grande gorge

It was a year that opened up Taos County for once and for all to what has followed: a helter-skelter, all-out invasion of land and culture; an in-migration of newcomers who are often insensitive to the needs, dreams, and realities of this fragile area. Hippies may not have realized it when they commenced pouring into northern New Mexico that spring, but they did break the ground and they set the stage for a Taos County invasion by the ugliest forces of the society they had hoped to escape from. Like Kit Carson many decades earlier, "they led the way."

On first arriving in Taos, I had an automatic deep sympathy for anyone rebelling against straight society. My experience in Taos changed all that. I quickly learned that rebellion without a political understanding and motivation is no rebellion at all. Just as I am certain that some Americans having no awareness of class struggle and the nature of imperialism went to Vietnam with so-called "benevolent" intentions, I am just as certain that many newcomers floundered sloppily into Taos County wanting to "do good." Yet their arrival simply became a further drain on the resources, both physical and emotional, of a people who could least afford that drain. Instead of promoting a new consciousness, many freaks wound up collaborating (if often unwittingly) with the powers-that-be to create the sort of confused, tense, and anarchical situation where commercial exploitation could grip the valley in a way that had been impossible before.

Fleeing the "middle-class values" of pampered childhoods, hippies poured into Taos in the early spring of 1970. They settled in individual crash pads, or in communes with names like The Five Star Farm, Morningstar, The Reality Construction Company, New Buffalo, Lorien, Lila, The Tree Frog Farm, The Hog Farm, The Family of God, and so forth. Some of these experiments in communal living and subsistence farming were financed by rich individuals whose wealth was generated by the profits of large corporations. A few freaks immediately offended their neighbors by washing themselves, their kids' diapers, their dishes, in streams and ditches from which downstream families drew their drinking water. Others offended a long-impoverished people by thoughtlessly trashing the middle-class aspirations of those people, not realizing that generations of oppression create a different value system from that generated by a lifetime of middle-class privilege.

They offended and frightened people by their arrogant "free love" and anti-family posturing, little understanding the importance of a closely knit family unit to the Chicano tradition — a strong familial structure being one of the few things that has held oppressed people together. Many freaks offended local residents by wearing filthy costumes — a sign of their rebellion — forgetting how important it can be for poor men and women to be at least clean and neat. Their attitude about dope offended, frightened, and angered a population already humiliated for decades by alcoholism born from the despair of poverty. Too, dope was an easy political bust and one that would half destroy the fledgling Chicano movement. Likewise, for minority kids at the bottom of the social scale, drugs, dope busts, the money, violence, and underworld energy involved, often mean the final step into a wasted life; whereas middle-class kids have money for bail and lawyers: the legal system is geared to defend their rights as representatives of the ruling class.

Perhaps the tension would not have exploded into the mini-war it released if there had not been serious political reasons for fanning the flames. But with César Chávez in California, Corky Gonzáles in Denver, and Reies Tijerina in northern New Mexico, the Chicano movement was in full swing and gaining momentum. Northern New Mexicans were banding together to fight for their land. A growing political awareness on their part had the power structure visibly frightened. In 1967 the governor had sent the National Guard into Tierra Amarilla. Neither Albuquerque nor Santa Fe had escaped the violence sweeping through urban ghettos in the late sixties, and there was more to come. As the third-poorest state in the union, New Mexico, with a majority "minority" population, was ripe for radical agitation. Besides Tijerina's land-grant movement, there were Black Berets in Albuquerque, a city one year away from a major riot. In Santa Fe, a powerful barrio group called La Gente was organizing against police brutality, starting a barrio clinic and Chicano school, and painting Raza murals on barrio buildings. In Tierra Amarilla an agricultural co-op, clinic, and graphics *taller* was run by men and women with an articulate left-wing social consciousness. Española was the home of *El Grito del Norte*, the powerful movement-pinto newspaper. In Taos, a Chicano group called Los Trabajadores de La Raza was trying to develop strong programs of social action. Several residents of the area, including my wife, Ruby, had been to Cuba, and were traveling around New Mexico giving slide shows on the Caribbean nation. The Taos Pueblo's sixty-year struggle for their Blue Lake land was coming to a head. Up in the San Luis Valley of southern Colorado, an area bordering Taos County, a lettuce and potato pickers' strike that would receive support from César Chávez's UFWOC union had begun. Hence there was much liberal and radical political ferment in an area that had been suppressed and exploited for many decades.

But when the hippie migration occurred, the community was seriously divided, and much of that groundwork for social reform in Taos was destroyed.

The Chamber of Commerce and affiliated organizations commenced the hysteria by calling the hippies dirty unwashed hordes. The school board jumped on the bandwagon, inciting students and their parents to riot with anti-freak broadsides. A right-wing, red-baiting Xeroxed newspaper appeared in many Taos business establishments. School kids, egged on by faculty members and other adults, formed vigilante squads that attacked freaks at random. And at a moment when this population had a good chance to truly understand the economic and social roots of their society, instead a kind of class and race war began.

During the first two weeks of April 1970, all hell broke loose. In Peñasco, dynamite destroyed a hippie van; a bomb blew apart a car in Vadito. In Pilar, flames destroyed a bridge to a freak community and six bullets were pumped through the front window of a nearby home. At the Ponce de Leon Hot Springs, where I had taken my first sunbath in Taos exactly a year earlier, a boy named William Elsea was shot in the leg; fire also gutted a house and a bridge at the Hot Springs. Twenty-five miles north of Taos near Questa, an apparent inter-hippie feud near the Lorien commune resulted in gunshot wounds. In Arroyo Seco, four men assaulted some longhairs and local craftspeople. A Chicano girl raped in El Prado claimed hippies had done it. And five bullets shattered the front windows of a new hippie General Store south of Taos proper.

The incidents multiplied. I have already mentioned my experience in the Pueblo gorge when my sister-in-law and I and our children were stoned from above. Other friends, middle-aged people recently moved to Taos from California,

had their car burned out. A friend on a bicycle was run off the road and almost killed. Another friend's car was forced off the road by some teen-age kids who then punched him in the face. Over in Mora County a group of local men shot and killed a commune dweller. A freak walking along the highway one night was beaten senseless by a carload of local teen-agers. My neighbor lost cattle to freaks who just killed them, bleeding and butchering the animals on the spot on the grounds that "everything belongs to God."

Down at the General Store to interview the leader of the Family of God commune in his office, I was puzzled by the surroundings. Out front, pacifist freaks wandered about scooping whole grains from colorful wooden bins, buying fertilized eggs cheap. But in the rear office, an FCC-licensed two-way radio set crackled, keeping in touch with various vigilante hippie vehicles patrolling the county and the communes, keeping an eye out for Chicano "bandits." Stacked in one corner were several high-powered rifles, most sheathed in expensive leather cases; one bookshelf contained many boxes of ammunition. The owner of this arsenal informed me that hippies could take care of their own.

And they could. A hippie, after his woman was allegedly raped by a local Chicano, shot the Chicano dead, then got off with a hung jury.

Several meetings sponsored by the White House Conference on Children and Youth were held in the old Taos courthouse. A cross section of the community spoke, anguish clouded everyone's voice. Some wished to kill the food-stamp program as a way of driving out hippies. A social worker named Jerry Ortiz y Pino protested: freaks constituted only 1 percent of the population using food stamps — it would be catastrophic for native New Mexicans if the program ended. A local woman nutritionist said, "For the first time in years people are being fed well." A vocational rehabilitation counselor expressed concern at "how some elements are using the Spanish-Americans as scapegoats." He was angered by some Chamber of Commerce statements saying, "The natives are against the hippies." "That is absolutely wrong," he said passionately, "and I don't happen to want to see any of our young people killed by hippies who are aroused by these statements. So we've formed a committee to help the kids realize they are being used to achieve the aims of others in the community. We

Pedernal, Abiquiu's special mountain, seen from Taos

All life and weather seem special.

don't want to see them sent to prison to advance the aims of other elements in the community."

It went on like that, back and forth, tragic to hear because nobody really knew how to analyze the situation. Racial tensions, as always, kept everyone from realizing how they were being duped. A group of artists had drawn up a useless petition against violence that they would publish in the newspaper. The editor of a freak sheet called *The Fountain of Light* said, "The violence problem is not a problem of hippies. Many people who have been beaten were not hippies. The fact is, if a person just wants to be different in this town, he's in danger. If he wants to wear a funny hat, he's in danger." An Anglo leather worker who had been mugged by local kids after they busted his shopwindow said helplessly, "All I wanted to do here in Taos was to work for an honest living—" An all-state high school football player retorted angrily, "Just how many hippies are actually trying to *work?*" A young woman cried, "I'm tired of being afraid to go out at night! I don't think this is America!" The maker of a counter-culture film called *Peace, Love, Taos—1969* shouted, "The country is totally falling apart, I assure you!" A calm resident of San Cristobal said, "All courts, all police, reflect the broad political atmosphere of the country, and so do ours. So I don't place any real blame on the courts. You can't mete out justice, nor can the police do their job, in an atmosphere like this." The minister of the Cañon Brethren Church, the Reverend Robert Salazar, opined, "I do agree we ought to care for our poor, and love our neighbors. But I don't believe in some of the political implications of this meeting. The more welfare you have, the more socialism you have, the more you'll be like the Soviet Socialist Republic. So I would suggest that right now we bring down an American flag, and with the atmosphere created by that we should all pledge allegiance to the flag."

But there was no flag to be found in the courthouse!

The meetings went on to accuse the press of being hysterical and one-sided, of publicizing violence in order to sell papers. A high school teacher told a Taos *News* reporter, "You allow yourselves to be used by the letters to the editor. They only fan the flames. And in your reporting, if it's a Chicano who does something, you use his name. But whenever somebody else does something, it's always alleged—and you don't use any names. . . ."

Elaborating on the subject, an old man stood up: "I want to ask if there is any law to prohibit such a thing as irresponsible journalism. I know we have freedom of the press, but isn't there a limit to it? I was born and raised in Arroyo Seco, I'm a Mexican-American. We came from a mixture of Spanish and Indian peoples. Now, I have heard some dirty words in my life, but the dirtiest words, they are in the English language. I have been called 'wetback.' I'm not afraid to say it. I'm not afraid to say either that the Anglos are a bunch of ignorants. They have just tried to cover up here. Laws are being abused by such things as they are doing here. Now . . . I have seen people going naked — that is called indecent exposure. But they call themselves Flowers of God. Well, I don't believe it. I have seen flowers in the field, all covered with dust, yet they still look beautiful to me. But I have never seen such filth as in those people who call themselves Flowers of God."

I sat through several meetings, feeling frustrated or outraged, or simply sad. People were emotional, on edge, and wearing blinders. They accused each other, nourishing suspicion and hate. Various factions involved fought each other to pathetic standstills. The only answer seemed to be an anarchical violence met by a counter-violence. The pacifists in the crowd could only offer an ineffective and childish sensibility yearning for "brotherhood." Nobody wanted to analyze the situation; probably nobody really could.

I emerged from the meetings astonished by the aimlessness of fiery emotions; and by the lack of a coherent framework — be it political, emotional, or social — that keeps us North Americans from being able to understand, let alone solve, our community problems.

By midsummer, however, the in-migration of freaks had slowed down considerably. You could see through the community's distress to stirring of honest social reform. Los Trabajadores de la Raza had initiated several projects that looked promising for Taos. In one, they were negotiating with Goddard College of Vermont, hoping to set up in Taos an accredited branch college serving the educational needs of poor Chicanos and Indians unable to go elsewhere. The institution would be called the Popé-Martínez College. Los Trabajadores had set up a nonprofit educational fund providing scholarships to the school.

Around this time a film crew arrived in town, hoping to make a documentary for educational TV about Taos, its people, the recent problems. Like most artists before them, the crew simply set up their equipment and started shooting. Los Trabajadores stepped in, asking what was in the movie for Taoseños. After some tension, the two groups reached an amicable agreement. If sold, a certain percentage of the film's profits would go into the Popé-Martínez educational fund. The crew also agreed to give Los Trabajadores all out-takes from the filming: the Chicano group planned to have local men and women put together their own film from these out-takes. In turn, Los Trabajadores would introduce the film crew to a cross section of Taoseños who had strong and important things to say about the local situation.

Los Trabajadores approached me for a favor, and I wound up one day leading the crew to Questa, where they shot an interview with José Cisneros. While José welded a horse trailer and showed them around his place and around Questa, he spoke about his community, life in the North, his struggle against the moly mine. The film makers recorded it faithfully, but in the end, obsessed with "objectivity," they made a muddled, wishy-washy movie having no clear point of view, just another rip-off of time, energy, trust, and dollars.

On other fronts, seeking to educate themselves better on international struggles, Los Trabajadores approached several women from the Taos area who had been to Cuba with the Venceremos Brigades. Though stating no position on Cuba, they sponsored a local slide show, feeling it would be important to learn something about that Caribbean island.

Also in town that summer were organizers of the San Luis Valley lettuce and potato pickers' strike. They talked with Taos County migrant workers. I attended several benefits on their behalf, and later inherited the clothes inventory of a bankrupt thrift shop, which a friend drove up to strike headquarters in Colorado.

Toward summer's end, Los Trabajadores played a significant role in bringing to Taos the Teatro Campesino, a people's theater born of the California farm workers' move-ment. The Teatro is one of the most accomplished — and funny — radical theater groups in this country. After the Town Council refused to let the Teatro perform for free in the Plaza, Los Trabajadores raised over a hundred dollars to rent the old Martínez Hall in Ranchos. They also arranged for the Teatro troupe to stay at the residence of film maker Dennis Hopper, a man whose donation had made rental of the Martínez Hall possible.

The Teatro's performance was one of the most creative and political acts that had occurred in Taos for a long time. It was the first theatrical performance I had viewed in Taos attended by a predominantly local crowd. Despite the outwardly conservative façade of Taos which had received much publicity during the recent conflicts, the Martínez Hall was packed to double its capacity. The audience laughed, cried, and after each act chanted along with the players: "Chicano POWER! Chicano POWER!" At the intermission, miffed by the strong politics, a few Anglos left the hall. But that only opened up spaces for more people to come in from outside.

Around the same time the Teatro Campesino had its success, the Taos Pueblo Indians started their final push toward realization of the Blue Lake dream — absolute ownership of 48,000 acres of mountainous forest land for which they had been fighting over sixty-five years. In their way stood Democratic senator from New Mexico Clinton B. Anderson's alternate Blue Lake bill. It would have made the land a special ranger district supervised by the Taos Indians, yet still in the hands of the Forest Service. Sick of swindling compromises, the tribe totally rejected any settlement except clear title to their sacred land. Anderson feared such a move would set a dangerous precedent — other tribes might demand the return of land stolen by the United States.

At the height of small euphorias generated by positive moves toward increased social awareness and changes, a state police undercover agent suddenly appeared in Taos with a grim tale:

A Chicano militia had formed in Taos and they had drawn up an assassination list of the richest and most powerful Anglos in town.

This rumor spread rapidly; I had heard it from a number of different people before I accidentally came across its source.

Snake crossing Rio Chiquito, Ranchos de Taos

Pueblo River gorge

The agent had gone to, among others, Dennis Hopper, informing him of the plot. The agent said Hopper was high on the assassination list, and that one of the film maker's friends, whom I'll call Ricardo — a very effective spokesman for Los Trabajadores — was a member of the militia that had drawn up the death list.

Playing on Hopper's fears, the agent embellished the plot to the point of absurdity. Yet in those days in Taos County people were uptight and would believe anything. The agent claimed the militiamen had purchased twenty four-wheel-drive vehicles, which they planned to outfit with automatic weapons. They then would drive into Taos, blow up the exits from town, and take over. Hopper's friend Ricardo, the Trabajadores spokesman, was prominently involved in this amazing scheme.

Hopper immediately arranged a meeting with the Trabajadores spokesman, asking why this man wished to kill him after the help he had given the Chicano group. As it happened, Hopper's rap was the first Ricardo had heard about the assassination list and the part he was supposed to have played in the making of it. But within a short time, Ricardo learned that his name in particular was connected to the grisly rumors circulating around town.

During the first week of October, two Forest Service signs near Taos were blown to bits with sophisticated explosives. Phone calls to local news media by unidentified persons said, "A response has been given to Senator Anderson in the form of two Forest Service signs."

On Tuesday night, October 27, a bomb exploded in the Peñasco Forest Service headquarters, twenty-five miles southeast of Taos, causing extensive damage. Later, the wire on a Forest Service corral was cut, allowing three horses to escape. They wandered onto a main highway, and two of the horses were struck and killed by a car.

Local officials called the bombings an outside job. Newspapers called them the work of Blue Lake supporters. Yet the name of the Trabajadores spokesman also appeared prominently in some theorizing. And, figuring himself about to be set up for a bust or worse, Ricardo moved from Taos, leaving Los Trabajadores bereft of important leadership.

No arrests for the bombings occurred. And in that kind of thing I always assume there's a chance at least some of the blasts were the work of provocateurs out to discredit both the Indians' Blue Lake claim and the local Chicano movement.

No Chicano militia surfaced, either. No assassination list went public. Nor were any of the Anglos supposedly on that list accosted. Obviously, no four-wheel-drive vehicles mounted with .50-caliber machine guns zoomed into town, and no exit roads disintegrated in a dynamite holocaust.

Weakened by paranoia, however, Los Trabajadores fell on hard times. The fragile unity of a town emerging from a nasty and confusing time was shattered: once again the ability of Chicanos, Indians, and Anglos to work together, trusting each other, was seriously impaired. Creative fledgling programs for social reform were discredited and rendered inoperable by a revivified atmosphere of racial violence.

But at the end of 1970 the Taos Pueblo won back its Blue Lake land. Honoring this great event, the Pueblo threw a feast for which a sacred buffalo was killed, and to which many outside political supporters of the Blue Lake struggle were invited. A Pueblo friend, Jim Suazo, asked me to attend the celebration with him. I balked, on the grounds that almost nobody from the Pueblo itself seemed to have been invited to this political chow-down. He pooh-poohed my misgivings, and led me to the banquet. Waiting in line for our buffalo, we were nearly deafened by a great clattering din of silverware clinking and glasses and chinaware clanking. Dignitaries at the long banquet tables trying to cut their buffalo steaks in a civilized manner with knives and forks were having a devil of a time making headway with the leathery meat. From U.S. Senator Joseph Montoya on down to the smallest political fish from the outside world, everybody grinned imbecilically and sweated profusely, trying to section the charred hunks on their plates, causing a small noisy earthquake with their hapless butchering endeavors.

Jim Suazo and I sat opposite each other at the end of one table. Winking at me, he grabbed his buffalo chunk in both hands and tore into it with his few remaining teeth. Seeing that, I grabbed my own hunk and lustily applied my crooked choppers to the task, until, amid the noisy clatter of that room, I suddenly burst out laughing.

Because it was absurd.

And because it was beautiful.

Sacred buffalo meat indeed!

I felt myself become a part of this county, its landscape, its historical processes in a single powerful moment, when a total stranger conferred upon me the same kind of compassionate compliment that the San Ildefonso man Ogwa Pi and his wife had conferred upon my mother forty years earlier by draping a string of turquoise around her neck while saying, simply and generously, "We like you."

The moment occurred in the spring of 1971 during a public meeting over the proposed Indian Camp Dam. A Bureau of Reclamation project authorized by Congress and part of a complex interstate water plan called the San Juan–Chama Diversion Project, the Indian Camp Dam was a sixteen-million-dollar "irrigation" venture, to be located east of Ranchos de Taos, creating a mile-and-a-half-long lake and retaining twelve thousand acre-feet of water. The Bureau of Reclamation and the New Mexico State Engineer advertised it as a project that might "save a dying culture"—by which they meant the rural Spanish-speaking farmers of the Taos Valley. Recognizing Taos for a terribly impoverished area, the government had agreed to subsidize 96.5 percent of the construction; local farmers would have to pay only 3.5 percent of the dam's building costs. They would also be responsible for half the maintenance costs of both the structure and the reservoir behind it. However, to make even that taxation feasible, Taos was being asked to form a conservancy district incorporating into the immediate reservoir service area about ten thousand people slated to receive "benefits" from the dam. And in New Mexico, a conservancy district is just about the most powerful political subdivision you can impose on a people, because such a district commands almost unlimited powers of taxation.

When I attended the meeting I knew almost nothing about the project or where people stood on the issue. But upon entering the old junior high auditorium, the community divisions were instantly apparent. Small farmers, exuding an air of polite mistrust, occupied one side of the auditorium. Across the center aisle from them sat a group almost entirely composed of Taos businesspeople, real estate brokers, bankers, and others identified with the commercial exploitation of the Taos Valley. And as soon as the meeting began, it became obvious that this latter group intended to sell the Indian Camp Dam to the small farmers using every trick in the book.

Given that the project's rhetoric touted benefits exclusively for those small farmers, the lineup seemed a trifle odd to me. The developers talked, cajoled, and wooed—addressing themselves primarily to that half of the room wearing dungarees and blue-jean jackets. "You are being offered a Cadillac for *free*," they said. But the ranchers smelled a rat in the upkeep and gas costs, and said nothing. They wondered who would really benefit more from the project—themselves or the "unselfish" town businessmen eagerly promoting the dam? They knew Taos desperately needed additional water rights to grow, and wondered if the fine print somewhere might not rob them of the little water they already had. Advised that the dam offered no greater water rights, but simply guaranteed a closer realization of rights already owned, the farmers had trouble understanding why they should have to start paying for water they had owned clearly for the past two hundred years.

A realtor who at that time happened to be chairman of the Taos Planning and Zoning Commission heaved up from his chair on the businessmen's side of the small auditorium and crossed to stand in front of the small farmers' section. He began by saying, "I won't really benefit directly from this—after all, I only own two acres." But later he told them: "Because of the dam, a number of new people will come here to live. And I don't think we should be selfish about it, we should let them come. In 1990 the United States will have a hundred million more people and a lot of them are going to want to come to Taos. A lot of them will be good neighbors, good citizens. And think about the recreation to be created by the new dam. People who come here to fish, they'll buy our products. They'll also buy homes. And of course, I'm interested in that."

Later, he concluded: "Understand, I have no personal interest in this water. It won't mean very much to me. But this is a chance we will never have again. So no matter what it costs, you must save the water for you and your grandchildren."

He sat down and silence followed.

I was so angered by the hypocrisy involved that I blew my cool in a way I had sworn I never would. Jumping up, I made

The central symbol in our lives

Sunrise, upper Taos Valley

an angry, emotional speech. I ran down county poverty statistics, applying them to various ethnic groups. I said that although there had been a countywide tourist-oriented economic "boom" ever since the Taos Ski Valley began operations in 1956, little of that affluence had touched the small farmers and poor people. After twenty-five years of development, the 1971 per capita income of $1,300 had less buying power, thanks to inflation, than the 1950 per capita income of $800. I quoted unemployment figures, and ran down welfare statistics and school dropout rates. I said that not much development money ever trickled down to local people; the little that did only kept them trapped in subsistence-level service-oriented jobs connected with the motel-hotel industry. I said county natural resources were limited and could support no more newcomers; hence, for each person entering the county, a corresponding local resident had to depart. I attributed the decline in Spanish-surnamed population to "progress, American style," and said that it sounded as if this dam project would actually benefit the tourism and development industries instead of small farmers. I said that despite the government subsidy, any added taxation on a populace earning very little would further weaken their fragile hold on the land.

Dam proponents had said the assurance of water would enable small farmers to change their cropping patterns from pasture and a few home vegetables to truck farms and orchards: I called that assumption crazy. First of all, at 7,000 feet, we had an absurdly short growing season. Fruit trees only produced on an average of twice every five years due to late-spring frosts. Garden seedlings were often frozen during the first week in June; mature plants usually bit the dust in early-September freezes. If poor farmers mortgaged land or houses to purchase the equipment for commercial endeavors needed to pay new water assessments, any natural disaster would wipe them out. And what kind of thinking believed that small farmers, living hundreds of miles away from all major distribution centers, could commercially market their crops? Taoseños couldn't even compete in their own valley with Safeway and Foodway! Not to mention the fact that if everybody grew crops for local sale, the bottom would drop out and you couldn't give away beans and tomatoes! Not only that, since conservancy assessments *had* to be paid, those taxes amounted to liens on property, an added indebtedness that would automatically make it easier for marginal people to lose their property — through foreclosures — to the commercial elements eager to develop it.

I said the dam and reservoir would attract more middle-class retirement- or recreation-oriented in-migrants, who'd buy land at inflated prices, driving up property values, increasing the taxation for the poor. Demand for middle-class services would further inflate taxes. The people of the valley had every right to suspect a government project, because almost every federal project in history had helped separate Spanish-speaking natives from their land. The Forest Service would oversee reservoir operations? — I lambasted the Floresta for its role in dispossessing original land-grant heirs of their terrain.

Breathlessly, digging an ever deeper hole, I continued. Who could tell what maintenance costs might be in the future? Any serious accident or repair costs would cripple marginal farmers. And as for the conservancy district: I knew next to nothing about such a structure, but it sounded as if its unlimited power to tax, condemn land, and initiate projects would be terribly dangerous for marginal farmers. And if a conservancy meant that control over local ditches would shift from individual communities to a powerful politically appointed five-man board, that could only spell disaster for an acequia system that had functioned as the unifying heart of the Taos communities for centuries. Finally, given the United States system, the sort of commercial growth coveted by the planning and zoning chairman could only mean the demise of small farmers, and hence of a Spanish-speaking culture in the Taos Valley. For all those reasons, I sensed that, instead of being a project to save a dying culture, the conservancy and the Indian Camp Dam were more likely to administer the coup de grâce to a vital, but struggling people.

Amen.

Sweating profusely, wishing I had kept my mouth shut in this room full of strangers, I sat down. Predictably, a man in the businessman's section said angrily that we didn't need any outside agitators in the valley. Another man challenged me directly, saying, "What gives you the right to talk? You came in here like everybody else and bought out a small farmer, didn't you?" I snapped back weakly that I had bought my house from an Anglo telephone lineman.

It was proceeding like that when a man on the small

farmers' side of the auditorium stood up, asking to speak. His name was Manuel Valerio. Turning to face me, he said, "I don't know who this man is . . . but he speaks the truth."

I was stunned. I wanted to embrace him for saving me, and for turning the tide of the meeting.

He went on, talking about his life in the valley, the changes he had seen, the way local folks always seemed to be left out, passed over, tricked, cheated. And after he had sat down, other men, most of them old and speaking quietly, stood up and explained that although they could use the water, they were afraid of the project. They wanted no more taxes. An earth-fill dam above their little communities seemed like tempting fate to make a disaster. Facts and figures on the costs were terribly vague. And what exactly was a conservancy district anyway?

Verbalized, the consensus among them seemed to be: "We fear that we are going to drown in all that extra water."

After the meeting, outside in the dark parking lot, many men from the small farmers' side of the auditorium shook my hand, congratulating me for my little speech. They were men called Andrés Martínez, Bernabé Chávez, Paul Valerio, Ralph Vigil, J. J. García, Jacob Bernal. Thanking me politely for my support, they invited me to attend their meetings. Some were part of a coordinating council that had originally gone to Washington, D.C., asking for San Juan — Chama diversion water. But now they were beginning to feel that the actual costs and the sociological implications would make it too expensive. Shortly thereafter, they withdrew from the coordinating council and formed the Tres Ríos Association in order to fight against the water "everybody wanted."

Six years have passed since that night. I have attended hundreds of meetings with those people. I have been to court hearings with them and to Interstate Streams Commission meetings, and to land and water events, demonstrations, and caucuses all over the North dealing with the struggle to protect land and water, communities, culture, roots. It has been the most valuable education I ever received. It has sent me into archives where I pored over tax records trying to understand the distribution of land and money and power in this county: it has forced me to go through legal statutes, and caused me to write amicus curiae briefs for the court. It has made me spend hours deciphering hydrographic survey maps. It has led me from tiny meetings in dusty schoolyards to giving speeches before the Lawyers' Guild at the University of New Mexico. Ultimately, it has led me to a fairly sophisticated layman's understanding of land and water politics in the Southwest. And it has given me a kind of overview of Taos Valley land patterns, who owns what and for what reasons. Most importantly, it has helped me learn the history of the North, not from the historians or the textbooks, but from the people who have lived it: friends, enemies, mentors — compañeros, amantes.

And it happened because a complete stranger had the generosity to stand up and legitimize my emotional diatribe by saying, "I don't know who this man is . . . but he speaks the truth."

The struggle against the Indian Camp Dam and the conservancy district deemed necessary to build the dam has been the most important struggle in the Taos Valley since I moved here. Implications of the conservancy district touch everyone in Taos. The sociological consequences would be the most radical and far-reaching of any changes planned for the valley.

Nobody knew back then, but over the years we have all learned what large irrigation or conservancy projects do to impoverished or subsistence areas. A definite tool of commercial progress, they have been used to develop large areas of the Southwest. Without a doubt they aid agribusiness people and industrial advancement. But they are hell on subsistence, marginal cultures. By forcing everybody into highly competitive cash economies, they weed out the weak from the strong. They efficiently take land from the hands of people unable or unwilling to commercially exploit it, and place it in the care of rapacious developers. In New Mexico's case, the dispossessed have usually been Spanish-speaking subsistence farmers whose culture doesn't necessarily venerate the so-called free-enterprise system. In a nutshell, then, conservancy and irrigation districts and large dam projects have often been oppressive to minority peoples.

Disguising the true nature of the Indian Camp Dam, a

Grazing in Las Colonias

Spring 1973

spokesman for the New Mexico State Engineer's office once said, "This project is an attempt on the part of the government to reverse the flight of the farmer from the land to the barrios of Albuquerque or Los Angeles. This is a project that is reserved for marginal farmers and is aimed at keeping them from boarding up their homes and leaving."

Citing examples to back himself up, the spokesman pointed to the success of the Elephant Butte Dam and irrigation project in southern New Mexico, saying, "These districts are in debt to the government, but they would have it no other way. They have farming where they had none before. Ask people near Elephant Butte and they will tell you the dam was a godsend that has made acequia farming into a prosperous business."

Prosperous for whom turns out to be the catch, however. For as soon as it researched the history of that project, the Tres Ríos Association learned that the Elephant Butte Dam had actually wiped out most Spanish-speaking farmers in south-central New Mexico.

One of the most thorough studies made of this tragedy was done by Middle Rio Grande Regional Conservator Hugh Calkins in 1936. Entitled *A Reconnaissance Survey of Human Dependency on Resources in the Rio Grande Watershed*, this report describes how, before Elephant Butte Dam, 70 percent of the 889 farms in the area were "owned by their operators," a large majority of whom were "Spanish-American." Cash production costs were low, there was little farm machinery in use, and only a few farms employed outside labor.

"Farmers satisfied the major part of their food needs from their own farms and, in addition, raised some surplus crops for adjacent markets. Farmers were not dependent upon distant and fluctuating markets, the need for high cash returns was not great. Transfer of farms was relatively infrequent. Stability and security, rather than speculation and insecurity, were characteristics of the area."

Elephant Butte Dam water, however, brought (as the Indian Camp Dam and conservancy district making the dam possible have proposed bringing to Taos) a changeover in cropping patterns which led to a highly commercialized type of farming. Cash expenditures for labor, machinery, irrigation water, and fertilizer skyrocketed. "Bankruptcy and the loss of farms became for the first time during those years not only a possibility, but a constant threat," according to Calkins. "Many of the original Spanish-American farmers, in the process of commercialization, were removed from their land through foreclosure."

Hence: "The irrigation project . . . was the instrument by which this essentially self-sufficing area was opened to commercial exploitation. The establishment—via this first investment—of a legal claim upon the resources of the area and the labor of its inhabitants, a claim which could not immediately be satisfied, led to the dispossession of the natives, and their replacement by American settlers financed by American capital. . . . The dispossessed Spanish-Americans, with no other means of livelihood than the sale of their labor, constituted the necessary cheap labor supply, supplemented by importation of labor from Old Mexico. Since they were now to a greater extent dependent upon cash, they constituted an additional market for consumption goods."

Calkins added: "The benefits of the high profits . . . were confined for the most part to a relatively small group of the entire population. . . . The largest proportion of the population, however, enjoyed no more ample livelihood than they had ever had."

And in conclusion: "Through the construction of a costly irrigation project . . . an additional land area of 100,000 acres was made available for agricultural use." But "the native population, unable to meet the new high cash costs, was in large measure displaced from 50,000 acres it had owned."

A noted sociologist, Dr. Clark Knowlton, more recently summed up the situation in this way: "Every major irrigation or water conservation project along the Rio Grande River, from the Elephant Butte Dam to the Middle Rio Grande Conservancy District, has been responsible for land alienation on an extensive scale. The Spanish-Americans have been replaced by Anglo-American farmers. Their subsistence agriculture has made way for a highly commercial, partially subsidized, and basically insecure agriculture, made possible by government programs. Little thought has ever been given to the rights and land use patterns of the Spanish-Americans in planning water projects in New Mexico and in neighboring states."

Given such evidence, the small farmers of the Taos Tres Ríos Association taxed themselves heavily to hire lawyers, do research, fly in expert witnesses to testify at court hearings, and obtain copies of transcripts for appeal, all in order to fight against a project the government and Taos area businessmen claimed had been designed specifically for their needs.

In the process, they learned that conservancies are nearly impossible to stop. The legal system is set up to make them inevitable. They can be initiated by a petition containing signatures of property holders owning one third the assessed value of the land within the boundaries of the proposed district. In this case, a handful of businessmen and absentee landowners could have thrown the district into court. A district can also be formed if any municipality — in this case the town of Taos — within the proposed district votes for it. Meaning that four town council members, elected by a population of roughly 2,500 people, could impose a heavy taxation district on an area of 10,000 people, 75 percent of whom had not voted the council members into office.

For a conservancy to be approved by the district court, its proponents must prove that all the land within the district will benefit. But "benefit" means simply that land values will rise in the area: sociological testimony is taboo.

It was a frustrating, emotional, often wildly comical five years. Court hearings were set, then postponed on absurd technicalities. Three hundred anti-dam small farmers packed the Taos County Courthouse at the first hearing. Perhaps fearing for his political future, the judge postponed the show on the grounds that district proponents had published legal notice of the hearing only in English: notice should have been published in Spanish too. Then he disqualified himself, and a Santa Fe judge took over. The next hearing was postponed when the wrong date for it was published in both Spanish and English in the legal section of the Taos *News*. A third hearing went by the boards when a major lawyer for the proponents dropped out the night before, claiming conflict of interest because he was also the lawyer for a group of land-grant heirs protesting the conservancy district. By then, the many small farmers who time and again had trekked faithfully to the courthouse were beginning to despair of a hearing ever taking place. Consensus among the legal committee and leaders of the Tres Ríos Association was that the proponents had deliberately fouled up procedures in order to exhaust the small farmers, kill public interest in the issue, and drain the financial and emotional resources of the Tres Ríos Association. Then,

finally, in empty courtrooms, they would make their case. Or have their fait accompli rubber-stamped by the legal system.

Eventually, however, a public hearing took place. Representing the proponents was the oldest law firm in Taos, composed of a board member of the First State Bank, the Assistant District Attorney, and a wealthy local attorney who flew his own plane to various cases around the state. Another member of their original team, a chairman of the Taos Centinel Bank board, had already unceremoniously retired from the case. Seated with the men was Paul Bloom, one of the cleverest water lawyers around, a Special Assistant to the State Engineer, and an architect of numerous water and water adjudication projects in the North.

Opposing this formidable lineup, representing the Tres Ríos Association, was a young legal-aid lawyer who had only recently become an attorney: this was his first big case. Aiding him on the hearing floor was a Tucson lawyer who had flown into Taos on no sleep the night before, a man briefed on the case about an hour before everybody entered the courtroom.

Although theoretically the hearing should have concerned only the formation of a conservancy district, most testimony concerned the Indian Camp Dam. The judge listened carefully to both sides, then reached a foregone conclusion by forming a conservancy district and appointing to its board five local politicos whose interests seemed directly in opposition to the valley's small farmers. In forming the district, however, the judge amended its boundaries illegally. And, in an appeal to the State Supreme Court based on that technicality, the Tres Ríos Association won a reversal of the district court decision: the conservancy was dissolved some five years after it first became a major issue.

Though based on a technicality rather than on the real reasons for opposing the district, the reversal was a triumph for the small farmers nevertheless, and a defeat for the Bureau of Reclamation, the State Engineer's Office, and local realtors, bankers, businessmen.

As of this writing, the issue is moot. Of course, the struggle is never over, and the dam, or a conservancy district, will no doubt be reactivated one day when people least expect it . . . or perhaps only after the old-timers — the guardians of this valley — are gone and the heritage of Taos County resides in the hands of less centered individuals.

Penitente cross east of Mabel Dodge Luhan house, Taos

Part VI

A FUTURE UP FOR GRABS

I traveled around the North, gathering impressions, listening to people, taking notes. I wrote articles for the New Mexico Review, *and clipped local newspapers and started files, in the process learning more about how the society of the United States functions than ever I could have learned in New York City. For some reason, the East had overwhelmed me; I could not deal with the scale of cities; I had found it difficult to run with people outside my own peer group. But in New Mexico, my relationships soon cut easily through class lines and occupations. I found I could connect personalities to the logistics of society; and the personal insights made everything very real; they focused motives and ambitions; they gave life to the human nature of history, exploitation, progress. The cop who gratuitously busted me for driving a hippie van had a sister who went steady with an alcoholic friend of mine —a mechanic, a rake, and a roustabout, who once drove a big Indian motorcycle from Rome Air Force Base outside Utica, New York, to Albuquerque in the dead of a bitter wartime winter. The town police chief read my last book and, if ever I wanted, he could tell me a thousand more stories about how cops function or dysfunction in the North. I can play badminton on Sundays with my lawyer, or take a sweat bath with a Navajo sculptor friend on Tuesday. As soon as I finish writing this I might play tennis with the small-town Nevada farm boy who runs the Plaza Theater. After that I might have a pizza in a joint run by a former Chicago social worker, a graduate of the University of Tel Aviv —we'll talk about Spinoza, Ping-Pong, the word "distinctive" in the seder ritual. If I want, I can stop at the mayor's furniture and hardware shop and shoot the breeze about politics. Or I can go by my neighbor's house to tell him his horse's time in my front field is up: he'll reminisce about his days in the Colorado mines. I can have coffee in the morning with the newspaper editor who's just agreed to pay me the enormous sum of five bucks for doing an editorial cartoon; I might trot over to Andrés Martínez's house—he is the head of the Tres Ríos Association— and we will talk either about the eight acres of barley he planted or about corporate financial philosophy in northern New Mexico. If I lose my cat, I'm liable to call across the river to the First Northern Savings & Loan president, who'll keep his eye out. If a cow dies in Phil Lavadie's field next door and it begins stinking up the community, that same neighbor (the president) will call me up, suggesting I lug some tires over and burn the putrid carcass before we all are fatally gassed. On my return from doing that, his father, a poet and singer of songs, is apt to be waiting in my driveway —we'll talk about the political history of Taos, and he'll sing me some old corridos opponents made up about each other while fighting to become county commissioners or senators or other types of political bigshots back in the thirties and forties. More on the business side of life, I can't get a Xerox in one stationery store without talking for an hour with Linda Trujillo about the social history of families in her Talpa neighborhood. And I can't buy carbon paper in another stationery store without going into the art of Zen and motorcycle maintenance with the woman who owns that store. I certainly can't pay my community water bill without having a long political discussion with Mrs. Gallegos, or listening to the songs she writes for the guitar; occasionally she tells me what it was like in the valley forty years ago. If I stop by the Taos Art Association to pick up my kid from his play rehearsal, I'm liable to have a one-hour discussion about plumbing with Bob Draper while he's trying to Roto-rooter a break in the main drain nearby. If I try to have a simple cup of morning coffee in Dori's Bakery, chances are I'll have a heavy discussion with Ed Devlin about rodeo roping or the real estate situation in Taos this* month. If I want to know about the personal history of my own little house, I can ask Eduardo Lavadie, who was born and raised in the house. If I want to hear the music of the great Chilean folk singer Victor Jara, I can listen to Marina García sing at La Cocina. Her family also owns the little Shetland pony I gratefully unloaded on them a few years back when I couldn't stand the beast any longer. When the Kit Carson Park skating pond freezes over come wintertime, I'm liable to play hockey there with the mechanic who keeps my VW running. A local woman of the valley, a fine adobe plasterer, is also in a political study group with me, and recently she returned from a three-week tour of China.

Or suppose I simply want to get right with the land: I'm within an hour of God knows how many different life zones. A half hour in one direction takes me across mesas, down talus slopes, into the Rio Grande Gorge. A half hour in another direction has me in pine forests or in lush mountain meadows through which picturesque trout streams indolently wander. If the chickadees desert my house in April, forty-five minutes up a dirt road brings me back to a cooler habitat they're inhabiting. And who knows how many snowball fights I've had in July, at elevations from which, using binoculars, I can still spot my house down there in Ranchitos, alongside the Pueblo River.

It's infinity in a grain of sand, this Taos, New Mexico. And the people are no different, and the society and the problems are no different from what I would encounter in Manhattan. But the scale is at a level that suits me, the noise at a decibel level I can manage.

And so I traveled around, moving easily among people as I had not in New York, and many gave willingly of themselves. And the land was always open, wide open and without trees, so that I could see all aspects of weather and landscape and wildlife. And I felt I had never been in so rich, or so threatened, a country before.

Without a doubt, the immediate future of this area is up for grabs. Despite the richness of cultures, the chaos here often defies imagination. Sometimes it seems as if Taos is caught in a riptide and is being helplessly dragged out to sea far beyond the reach of helping hands or benevolent philosophies. Although the population seems to remain fairly static at about nineteen thousand people, in the past eight years I have watched a phenomenal amount of building take place. The construction, the new developments, the commercial aspirations of the valley reflect the relentless in-migration of middle-class people, who are rapidly displacing the subsistence poor. Local cultures suffer because of this influx, and the land is taking it on the chin, from fragile irrigated valley pastures to the slopes of Wheeler Peak.

Permits are needed now to enter designated wild areas, and the wilderness designation itself often seems like a joke. On trails leading to Williams Lake, just below Wheeler Peak, the average backpacker is lucky not to be caught in a traffic jam: and the chipmunks are so civilized they are liable to mug him or her for their candy bars. I have stood on twelve-thousand-foot-high ridges in the Sangre de Cristos unable to see forty miles southward because of smog drifting up from Albuquerque, east from the Four Corners power plants, and in from the Taos Valley directly below. I have hiked into the beautiful Latir Lakes an hour north of Taos, and found them surrounded by garbage dumps, a hundred Boy Scouts slaughtering trout, or noisy out-of-staters guzzling beer. Snowmobiles and motorcycles unleash a constantly irritating engine noise high in the hills, and their trails are everywhere. Exploratory mineral cuts scar the mountains around Questa, and a poisonous dust from the moly mine's tailings lake often blows over that picturesque town. Several times, when I have been fishing the Red River below the mine, the water has suddenly been colored opaque lead from a line break above. To aid public relations, the mine is constantly stocking the river with fish, even as it petitions the government for permission to dump its wastes into the wild river section of the Rio Grande.

Citizens of Red River wish to build a transmountain road to the Taos Ski Valley, linking the two vacation resorts. Taos Ski Valley developers want to double the size of their village, placing a new town at the source of a river, the Hondo, which would further threaten the water supply feeding several downstream farming communities: Valdez, Des Montes, and Arroyo Hondo. Already that stream, lined as it is with camping areas, and polluted by sewage that often bypasses inadequate vacation-home systems, is one of the more polluted rivers in the state.

The county has, in the past, been decimated by carelessly constructed logging roads and by badly managed timber cutting. Erosion is a problem. Bald, formerly forested land at high elevations means that the snowmelt now occurs earlier and faster than in former times, contributing to erosion and making for irrigating crises during the summer. In Taos Canyon's Valle Escondido, dozens of tiny trout ponds built for summer tourists sap the Rio Fernando during the dry season, creating irrigation problems down below in the Cañon section of Taos. As irrigated valley land is taken from agricultural production for housing developments and shopping centers, as it is paved over or bisected by new roads, the water table sinks at an alarming rate, and private wells must be drilled ever deeper. New businesses like the Holiday Inn, with their hundreds of toilets, place a further drain on limited water supply, making the lack of water a major crisis. At the same time that the Forest Service hurts small ranchers by reducing grazing in order to maintain a "healthy forest," it promotes commercial enterprises such as mining and timbering, which put enormous pressures on our resources. In particular, the Floresta promotes tourism — that is, the influx of money-toting, and often super-destructive, people — an industry that compromises the natural environment as no cow or sheep ever could.

It is fascinating to watch the agitation in the valley. And although progress, American style, is frightening, I also immensely enjoy being alive in this rich and overwhelming territory. The scamming is ridiculous, ludicrous, vital. A corporation has bought the Ponce de Leon Hot Springs of Llano Quemado, wishing to make them into a resort. The same corporation recently tried and failed to finance a Ramada Inn with Taos town tax-free municipal-industrial bonds. Everywhere sun-heated houses are going up. Taos has become a center for solar technology. A recent weekend-long solar energy fair at the Holiday Inn was a great success. Other cheap-shot housing projects defy credulity: how can supposedly semi-sensitive human beings slap such banal and shoddy hovels onto this lovely land? Dozens of such quickie projects, each touting many units, have gone up in my time. Along the major highway, PDQs, gas-o-mats, and fast-food stands pop up overnight. Operation Breakthrough and other flimsy government housing insults are marching across the landscape like Sherman through Georgia. A new high school, a new junior high school, a new courthouse have sprouted since my arrival in Taos. I would venture that at least two dozen gas stations have gone up since I reached town. A highway bypass has been added, golf courses have been built, and — thanks to the middle-class onslaught — tennis has become a popular valley game. You can play at the Sagebrush Inn courts; the town is building public courts at a former sewage-plant site; and an operation called the Tennis Ranch offers elite dining alongside courts protected by a garish green-and-white bubble making winter games possible. Too, speaking of upper-class diversions, I know of at least four people in the valley who raise prestigious, and enormously valuable, Arabian horses.

In the old days, the Catholic Church held monopolistic spiritual sway in the valley. Now the county is so rich in spiritual diversity it hums. Penitente brotherhoods still exist. Communes, like New Buffalo, have survived the rise and fall of the hippie scene. In hills between Arroyo Hondo and San Cristobal, the Lama Foundation offers Sufi dancing on Sundays and an eclectic life of hard work and worship otherwise. Peyote meetings of the Native American Church take place regularly. The hills and valleys are riddled with gurus, some of them charlatans, others eminently respectable. Allen Ginsberg, Baba Ram Das, and Roshi Baker have been here and gone. Dozens of recent locals make trips down to Alamogordo for aura adjustments. Others here are experimenting in mind control and bio feedback. Scattered enclaves of newcomers believe in pyramid power. And in the past eight years the sightings of flying saucers have quadrupled.

Pueblo religious fiestas, such as September's San Geronimo and the Christmas deer dances, are as strong and as beautiful as ever. Outside the reservation, Jehovah's Witnesses are proliferating like rabbits: and rare is the week when clean-cut Mormon lads wearing impeccable three-piece suits don't walk up my driveway seeking a literary convert. Evangelists work the town regularly, set up tents, preach and convert and make money, and then skedaddle. Every now and then funky little carnivals and traveling circuses pitch camp, next door to the rodeo grounds, or maybe right beside the local KOA

Pueblo River gorge, near Los Córdovas

View north from the Pueblo River gorge

Kampground, which is usually so full of Brobdingnagian Winnebago touring buses it groans. There are folks in town who'll sponsor a Share Fair, a benefit carnival whose proceeds go to starving orphans in India. At the same time, another group will be busy throwing a benefit dance to aid the defense of a local northern New Mexican radical recently incarcerated by a New York grand jury for refusing to testify about aspects of the Puerto Rican independence movement. It is a fact that, per capita, more people from Taos than from any other American town or city have visited the People's Republic of China. Given the number of seders that take place here each spring, I would venture to say that we have more seders, per capita, than any other U.S. population center. For more local folks, feasts called cabritos, involving the barbecueing of kid goats, continue to flourish. Of course, Zen weddings are popular; other couples exchange vows at dawn on the mountaintops; and traditional old Spanish weddings still occur — guitarists play entriegas, and dances follow.

On Highway 68 an incredible traffic jam endures from early June through early September. And the roads are as potholed now as when I arrived: corrective measures, thanks to limited funds, are always stopgap.

As in any improverished area, alcoholism is rampant. Smack and cocaine are problems in and out of the schools, not to mention pot, liquor, and a thousand variations on the upper-downer syndrome. Grotesque car accidents, usually involving strung-out teen-agers, are much too frequent: the death toll in Taos County is abnormally high. Other kinds of violence, exacerbated by racial tensions, occasionally flare up. Everybody has a gun, and the weapons are often used. A friend of mine once raced around the Plaza busting plate-glass windows to draw the cops because some kids were trying to beat him up and rape his girl friend. Seeking revenge, he drove out to where his tormentors lived, and shotgunned their automobiles. At Friday-night boogies, beatings and an occasional parking-lot rape have occurred often enough to be called almost common. The father of a Pueblo friend was beaten to death with rocks one night. Each year sees a sensational murder case or two. A father from Amalia executes his three kids while they are watching television; in Questa, three men from outside the state rape and shoot up a family amid overtones of witchcraft; in Taos, a man's mistress executes his wife and small child; and a respected artist shoots a homosexual in the stomach after the gay threatens to molest the artist's child.

I lock my car as carefully here as I would in New York City: still, it has been ripped off three times. A good friend lost all his tools in broad daylight when he left his truck parked for five minutes before a restaurant. While an artist friend was out sketching primitive countryside, all four tires were stolen off her parked car. Burglaries are endemic: sometimes rifling houses seems to be the biggest industry in town. Fluorescent red signs proclaiming NO TRESPASSING, PRIVATE PROPERTY, BEWARE OF DOG have proliferated as class gaps widen, the middle class becomes more predominant, and paranoia flourishes. A neighbor recently complained: "In the old days, when you killed a pig, all the neighbors would come around and help and you gave them some of the meat. Nowadays, when people are slaughtering an animal, they do it in private, they don't want anybody else to know, they don't want to share."

The art colony is as strong as ever. Fritz Scholder shows here, R. C. Gorman and Andrew Dasburg live in town. Larry Bell is building a studio one block from the Plaza. Larry Calcagno has a home here. A recently opened gallery has Frank Stellas and Andy Warhols on its walls. The writing colony is expanding unconscionably. Respected old-timers like Frank Waters, Joe Foster, and Victor White are still around. Newcomers, such as mystery writer Ron Faust, ex-southwestern football hero Doug Terry, and local talent Reggie Cantu, promise to enhance the literary reputation. In April 1977, Dorothy Brett was still alive and living on the mesa north of town. Film star Dennis Hopper purchased the enormous Mabel Dodge Luhan mansion some years ago.

The mélange of personalities is crazy. A bearded freak lives in an Arroyo Hondo cave on a trust fund. Today's carpenter was in New York arbitrage yesterday: he used to spend his vacations bone fishing with a fly rod in Florida. A former *Life* photographer raises goats and builds furniture. A man whose father once embalmed a whale in San Diego buys antiques in Europe and sells them around New Mexico. A woman who serves catfish dinners in a local restaurant spent half her life in Pakistan and Uganda, and also danced with the Folies-Bergères. A former high-powered Denver stockbroker just got a job as a Headstart teacher at the Taos Pueblo.

There is a strong gay scene in Taos and plenty of middle-class alcoholics. Motorcycle gangs stir things up on a regular basis. Members of Corky Gonzáles's Denver-based Crusade for Justice have been known to take their R and R in the valley. Two months ago I saw the film *Bound for Glory* flanked by California members of AIM.

A local theater group will do Tennessee Williams plays. Kids from the Taos Art Association will put on a complex, stylized Chinese play such as *Lady Precious Stream.* Another group of wacky players perform for free in Kit Carson Park. Every year Los Comanches dancers from Talpa and Ranchos and Llano Quemado commemorate old Indian fights. At Christmastime many rooftops and driveways are decorated with luminarias — paper bags holding candles stuck into sand: and a nostalgic sense of the past is overwhelming.

On the one hand, much farmland is being taken out of production by newcomers, by the helter-skelter development. On the other hand, everybody has a garden. In summertime, the valley is gorged with vegetables. Next to the new courthouse, a farmer's market functions well from July through September. And three organic-food stores have come to successful fruition since I arrived. A few enterprising, and not a little masochistic, individuals, such as my novelist friend Stan Crawford in Dixon, actually make a living selling vegetables: he supplies Santa Fe restaurants with choice greenery. And by the time this is published, his fourth novel will have been released.

Everybody is on a hustle. An ex-D. A. from Oklahoma is making it as a jeweler. A former newspaper reporter from New Orleans is mass-producing log splitters. A former Hollywood director and scriptwriter lives in an eighty-five-dollar-a-month adobe and drives a rattletrap pickup. A marine biologist, now a potter, occasionally leaves town to attend such events as an acaleph conference in Tokyo.

An eight-team Little League is alive and well in Taos. In the past five years summer softball — men's leagues, women's leagues — has grown in popularity: two or three evenings a week, during July and August, games are being played simultaneously on eight diamonds around town. On the same day you can go from watching the old-fashioned shearing of a rancher's sheep out on the Carson mesa west of the gorge, to viewing the latest Bergman, Antonioni, or Woody Allen movie at the Plaza Theater. The Taos Art Association's new theater shows classic films — Garbo, Bogart, James Dean. Or it will sponsor a local talent show featuring, side by side, a group from the Pueblo reciting poetry while doing Indian sign language for the verses and a recently arrived freak walking a tightrope across the stage. Some town restaurants offer traditional Mexican foods. Others are so heavy on the sprouts and organic vegetables you can practically hear the vitamins crackling! A few eateries specialize in snails and two-inch-thick beefsteaks.

Of course, cable television has come to the valley. An FM radio station recently began broadcasting. A palmist on the highway south of Ranchos will tell your fortune. One of the last of the valley's surviving sheepmen drives an eight-thousand-dollar Chrysler. The son of an itinerant sheepherder graduated from Harvard Law and works for the government in Washington, D.C. Some local musicians, like Vito Trujillo, who left Taos years ago to score a living in Los Angeles, have returned to Taos because they can now turn a dollar here. But many other locals must leave, because there are no jobs for them in town, there is no land left they can afford to live on. And when he returned recently from the East, a friend of mine who grew up here said he never wanted to return for good, because it hurt him too much — emotionally, spiritually — to see the disintegration of his family, of the strong community structure that once held sway here, keeping a sense of things together.

It's a struggle. The process of supplanting a solidly rooted culture with a more transient, less committed society is painful to watch. Many of the middle-class people make Taos an ever more interesting and vital place to live in. Yet ultimately I cannot sympathize with the ethic they bring. Middle-class, semi-dropout capitalism, for all its gaudy plumage, will turn this valley into just another paranoid, money-grubbing boardwalk — a mountain Las Vegas, Atlantic City, Tahoe, in miniature. Dusty, choked, garbled, overpopulated, shrill, and angry — the newcomers will wonder where the magic went. "How is it," they'll stammer, "that we created just another place made up of individuals out for themselves? How is it that we allowed Taos community patterns to become lost in a powerful rush to grab everything while the grabbing was good — ?"

Pueblo land, near Arroyo Seco

Part VII

A VIEW FROM THE HILLS

I am greatly moved by the old-timers. Many of them are not particularly political. But they are quite powerful and together people, and although they are angry, they are also patient. They have a great respect for each other, even if enemies. And, although many of them have been seriously exploited all their lives by an unfair system, they have an incredible sense of humor. They are not going to take anything lying down; they can be enraged and even reach for guns sometimes. But they have an enormous generosity of spirit about life, and a tolerance of human beings and human foibles —if not of the messes that human beings cause. And they have a rhythm that understands the nature of the long haul. There is neither bitterness nor hatred in their understanding of life. And there is a certain humility that forges dignity instead of weakness.

On certain levels, these people are as confused and convoluted as all of us. Yet at the heart of their often traumatic daily lives they have a perspective and clarity of heart that have been enormously seductive to me. Contact with them has calmed me down. And it has helped me gain back a sense of humor and a real love of life that I was in danger of losing. They taught me how to be tolerant again. They taught me how, in the thick of any fight, to also enjoy myself ... despite worldwide hunger,

poverty, war, and all the other insults to humanity. They taught me much about the power and the glory of everyday people.

About Walt Whitman, Mike Gold once wrote:

Walt dwelt among the masses, and from there he drew his strength. From the obscure lives of the masses he absorbed those deep affirmations of the instinct that are his glory. Walt has been called a prophet of individualism, but that is the usual blunder of literature. Walt knew the masses too well to believe that any individual could rise in intrinsic value above them. His individuals were those great, simple farmers and mechanics and ditch-diggers who are to be found everywhere among the masses —those powerful, natural persons whose heroism needs no drug of fame or applause to enable them to continue; those humble, mighty parts of the mass, whose self-sufficiency comes from their sense of solidarity, not from any sense of solitariness.

A credo, then, honoring the gift of community my neighbors have so unselfishly shared with me:

Because they are stealing from us our land, our food, our schools, our languages, our values, our stories, our reli-

gions, and all the good things in our white, black, brown, and red cultures, we are at war with them.

Because they are taking from us our real music, and the future of our children, we are at war with them.

Because they are trying every day to brainwash us, with their electronic media, into a lobotomized state of bovine passivity, we are at war with them.

Because they are transforming our mountains, our plains, our valleys, and our rivers into security lamps, air conditioners, and a trillion other poisonous consumer items, we are at war with them.

Because they are destroying entire continents in order to embalm the American spirit, from Tierra del Fuego to Point Barrow, we are at war with them.

Because their pursuit of growth simply for its own sake is, as Ed Abbey once put it, "the ideology of the cancer cell," we are at war with them.

Because they are emasculating Pueblo Indians and black ghetto youths as well as befuddled white executives and money-hungry superstars, we are at war with them.

Some of us choose iron and steel to wage this war. Some of us learn how to throw bombs and aim bullets. Some of us consider poetry a weapon. Some of us believe that the houses we live in and the fields we irrigate are weapons. Some of us plant trees instead of destroying them, and those trees are weapons. Some of us remember Diego Rivera and paint street murals to bring alive our faltering neighborhoods, and the murals are weapons.

Many of us don't know how to protect our land or our spiritual territory with guns. Nor can we make the bewildering legal system bend a trifle in our favor. And electoral politics are a joke. But no matter: we are forever bound and determined to wage this war with our own humanity.

Our gesture against this annihilating republic shall be a deer dance, a photograph of that mountain, a picket line, an understanding of Marx, a dream of Cuba, real hugs for our children, corridos about Zapata and Tijerina, and a true sense of being alive.

It's all important; it all counts; we're all in this together.

Only the real people can save us from this doom our society is weaving.

We absolutely refuse to enter the future as just another trenchant historical footnote in somebody's best-selling book about broken treaties or dodo birds!

Beginning this memoir, I had plans to write about many personalities. At the end, now, I wish to speak about a single man. In him I find the best qualities of the most important people on earth.

From its inception, until just recently, the president of the Tres Ríos Association has been Andrés A. Martínez. A short, stocky man with wavy gray hair, a mustache, and a seemingly inexhaustible supply of energy and patience, at eighty-one he shows no sign of slowing down. A widower who recently remarried, he lives in a trailer with his new wife, Jeannette, tends a garden, irrigates a small back field, and this year planted eight acres of barley behind the Cañon Headstart building. Recently, he broke an arm slipping on winter ice. Next day, we drove an hour and a half south to a small town called Hernandez for an important land and water rights meeting to which nobody besides ourselves went. The day after that, Andrés drove with his friend Pacomio Mondragón down to Houston, Texas, to fetch a horse trailer. When they returned, Andrés planned to visit Albuquerque for several days, demonstrating at court hearings featuring a group of Chilili land-grant heirs attempting to salvage the remains of their grant from developers. At the last moment Andrés could not go, because, while plowing that eight acres of land for barley, his wallet fell from a pocket, and he spent two days on his hands and knees in the field locating it. Last year, while plowing a different field, his clothing caught accidentally in a mechanism, the clutch slipped on the tractor, and the machine was dragging him around the field when a neighbor spotted his predicament, ran over, and saved his life.

Those things don't faze Andrés. Neither did the endless delays and organizing problems inherent in keeping the Indian Camp Dam struggle alive. Andrés has seen it all. He has led a varied life of intense struggle and richness, most of it connected to the land. He has followed lambing from southern Arizona to northern Idaho; he has lain in the hills at night listening to his father's coyote scare gun firing. He once ran a Navajo trading post in Ramah, New Mexico, and worked in the copper mines of Colorado. Wandering all over the Southwest, he worked at various jobs, attended and taught school, and in 1946 finally returned to his home town, borrowing enough money to start a small dairy farm, a business he ran for years until rubbed out by the large chain dairies down south.

Andrés is a gentle and humorous man, and honest enough to command the trust of a great many people whose immediate futures were jeopardized by the conservancy district. Originally one of those who traveled to Washington asking for the water, when he realized the price that might have to be paid, he had the courage to change his mind, even though the idea of a large reservoir in a county where barely twelve inches of rain fall annually was almost impossible to oppose. Andrés has driven tirelessly around the North, recruiting aid and information; he has sorted sincere offers out from the charlatan advances; he has slalomed neatly through all sorts of political skulduggery and attempts to wreck the Tres Ríos Association by defaming his judgments. He has taken a thousand small and large insults, and persistently come back for more, attacking and learning with patience, dignity, tenacity. He has tirelessly driven to the capital with friends and members of the Tres Ríos Association, appearing in person before the bureaucratic powers-that-be, letting them know that he and the resistance he stands for are alive and well in the North. He has even suffered the indignity of having his own state senator throw him bodily out of the senator's office when Andrés challenged that man to take a stand on crucial issues.

Andrés laughs easily: his eyes twinkle when he says, "You know? I wouldn't trade a college education for everything I have learned these last six years."

Turning then, and gazing up into the hills, he remarks to me, "I would like to climb up there this summer, one last time, and look over the valley again. I would like to see it just once more before I'm through, all this territory here, all my land."

I would like to go with him, seeing the terrain as he sees it with all those layers, all those struggles — the people, the stories, the farms. I would like to see that sagebrush terrain between Talpa and Cañon as it used to be, as Andrés remembers it from his childhood, all green with grass and under cultivation as far as the gorge. And I would like to see the lacrosse-like games of chueco between villages as Andrés used to see them. And I would like to see the horse races they used to have on the mesa, especially the one where a smart hustler tethered a mare in heat just beyond the finish line for his stud to gallop to — and won the race. I would like to see the wild burros down in the gorge that his father once rode over to the railhead at La Servilleta. And I would like to see his little dairy farm and his cattle grazing on all that green land that is fast becoming ugly subdivisions.

Already the valley land, from any high vantage point I choose, has become a thousand times richer for me. When I survey it, I see the map of what has happened here; now I connect history to this landscape. When I spot Abiquiu Mountain far to the south, I know that these days people are organizing to stop a Corps of Engineers project at the Abiquiu Dam which may forever destroy their way of life. When I view the mesa just above Pilar, I think of bright stars, and the barking of coyotes outside the window mingling with black tobacco and blissful peace. I also know that in the foothills of Picuris Peak are mines where people still get tierra blanca for whitewashing adobe walls. When I look at Los Córdovas, I think of that sewage-plant struggle, and of Otto Pitcher's pond where the ruddy ducks gather in the fall, and of the Trujillo brother who froze to death one bitter January night. When I reconnoiter the Ranchos-Talpa Valley, I see the patterned pastures of small farmers who have been at the heart of the conservancy district fight; and I remember how the valley looked from under Justin Locke's irrigation waterfall. Swinging north to my own Upper Ranchitos community, I think of the acequias on which I have worked, and of the wedding receptions at Sebastian's now defunct bar, and of the church bells on that quiet autumn morning when Bernardo Trujillo died. North of town, my eyes sweep across the Pueblo, remembering the Blue Lake struggle. I also recall a Christmas meal out there, in the unelectrified dark: the mud apartment buildings were faintly lined by new snow — a scene so lovely it caused chills. Farther north lie Arroyo Hondo, Valdez, and Arroyo Seco; their land and water are threatened by the expansion of the ski valley up above. Beyond, the road aims north through

Thicket in Rio Grande gorge

The most beautiful place on earth

sage land and piñon forests, traveling to Costilla and beyond, the same road that we descended eight years ago, the road that channeled us into this wide, desperate, lovely valley, a place that was without history for us then, only a beautiful spot with traffic jams — and then our time began.

I would see other things from the hills, standing beside my aged friend who can look at this valley with love and good humor, with anger and purpose. Against the sagebrush plain below, and the narrow gash of Rio Grande Gorge, and the soft hills beyond, I would see the statue of my great-grandfather Anatole Le Braz in a park at St.-Brieuc, listening to a folk tale told by a Breton woman. And I would picture my mother at her bedroom window that first night in New Mexico, saying, "I can see all the stars in heaven. Oh I am happy, happy, happy!" And I would see my father on that misty morning at the old Mastic house, smoking a pipe, leading me out to check on his traps. And I would see my grandfather, standing on the aft deck of an old sailing vessel threading its way gingerly through Cape Horn icebergs, reeling in an albatross.

Their roots, and the roots of similar folk, are here.

In me.

In Bill Davis.

In Andrés Martínez.

In many people of this high valley, this threatened mesa country.

And those same roots are in the mist that rolls off Blue Lake and travels downstream, over the Pueblo apartments, along the river past my house, and into the gorge beyond Los Córdovas. Ancestors from the past, and unborn spirits from a future time . . . tracing, with such great feelings of love, the bittersweet flow through all these good and bad times, through this landscape whose eternal meanings are derived from the human heart —

Through this home.